PARLIAMENTARY PROCEDURES SIMPLIFIED:

A Complete Guide
To
Rules of Order

By
LUCILLE PLACE
Illustrated

A World of Books That Fill a Need

Frederick Fell Publishers, Inc.
NEW YORK

Library of Congress Cataloging in Publication Data

Place, Lucille.
    Parliamentary procedures simplified.

    1. Parliamentary practice. I. Title.
JF515.P693   060.4'2   76-16466

Library of Congress Catalog No. 76-16466
ISBN: 0-8119-0269-2
ISBN: 0-88391-049-7 (Paper)

For information address:
Frederick Fell Publishers, Inc.
386 Park Avenue South
New York, New York 10016

Published simultaneously in Canada by
Fitzhenry & Whiteside,
Limited, Toronto

2 3 4 5 6 7 8 9 0

Manufactured in the United States of America

Parliamentary Procedures Simplified:

A Complete Guide
To
Rules of Order

Dedicated to

The memory of my Dad and Grandpa

Henry Clay Cutliph, Sr.

Henry Clay Cutliph, Jr.

and to the future of my children, Jimmy, Charmian, and Terry

and especially to my grandson, "Gib"

" . . . . . with Liberty and Justice for ALL . . . ."
Hopefully, future generations can make these words a reality.

Lucille Place

ACKNOWLEDGMENTS

I want to express my thanks to *Richard S. Kain,* past president of the American Institute of Parliamentarians for designing the CHART used in this book; and to Robert D. Tucker, a mechanical engineer and one of my former students, who made the CHART available for practical use.

My thanks also to the faithful members of the American Institute of Parliamentarians who are responsible for the continued inspiration and encouragement that motivated me to write this book.

And especially to my very patient and understanding husband, Vernon.

ACCOLADES

"PARLIAMENTARY PROCEDURE SIMPLIFIED is a new approach in learning this subject. The book is written in understandable language and uses the most commonly used motions. The Motions Chart illustrates procedure and a good, workable understanding is given in the question and answer section."

Lester L. Dahms
Executive Director
American Institute of Parliamentarians

—

"I am pleased to see that Lucille Place, a leading American parliamentarian, has finally accepted the challenge of writing a new, simplified approach to parliamentary law. Her book is clear because her thinking is clear."

Dr. Darwin Patnode
Chairman of the Accrediting Committee
Past President
American Institute of Parliamentarians

—

"PARLIAMENTARY PROCEDURE SIMPLIFIED by Lucille Place is a short cut to understanding the rules for democratic meeting procedure. Organization men and women would do well to consult this book first if they wish to become more effective in a short time in their participation in meetings."

Richard S. Kain, CPP
Past President
American Institute of Parliamentarians

CONTENTS

PART III—ANSWERS TO THE QUESTIONS ON PARLIAMENTARY SITUATIONS

PART IV—THE CHAIRMAN

PART V—GLOSSARY

INTRODUCTION

During 1976 we celebrated the 200th birthday of our country. This very special occasion heightened our sense of gratitude for living in a nation where we may enjoy freedom of speech and the absolute right to exercise that liberty. Yet, while we gave our thanks, we were also aware that during these years we have simultaneously experienced oppression and chaos.

I have personally observed and experienced both of these extremes during my lifetime—the freedom and the chaos. The revelations born of these experiences, as well as my 26 years of almost continuous research in the field of parliamentary law, has convinced me without equivocation that if we are truly to fulfill the principles of freedom that Thomas Jefferson wrote about when he composed the Declaration of Independence, a fourth "R" must be added to our educational process: Readin', Ritin', 'Rithematic, and RULES.

Although most individuals claim to use the accepted parliamentary authority, *Robert's Rules of Order,* few appear to have learned the basic concept of the *Rules.* Unfortunately, too many people believe that everyone else took a course in parliamentary procedure at school and, therefore, are educated in the mechanics of meetings. This, of course, is a myth. The truth is that there are very few who have been schooled in the process and there are very few who are prepared to participate or preside at a meeting, including legislative sessions from the local to the national levels.

Our most erroneous assumptions are applied to the educational and legal professions. We assume that educators and lawyers emerge from universities and law schools well versed in parliamentary procedure without acknowledging the difference between the practice of law *per se*, and the practice of parliamentary law. There is an important and significant distinction that must be made between these two bodies of knowledge, yet I have found few law schools or any other schools throughout the country that offer even a short course on the subject. This lack in our educational process accounts for the chaos within our system, for WHEN RULES ARE MADE UP AS WE GO ALONG, THEY ARE INCONSISTENT AND INEVITABLY CAUSE CONFUSION.

The purpose of this book is to clear up that confusion; to instruct you in the rules for most effectively exercising your freedom of speech; to teach you how to have your voice and all voices heard; and to offer you a simplified course in parliamentary procedure.

Lucille Place

Part I

WHY PARLIAMENTARY PROCEDURE?

What is Parliamentary Law?

My young daughter recently asked me, "Mother, why do we need parliamentary procedure?" I explained to her that "parliamentary procedure has the same effect at a meeting as the traffic laws have on the streets. If you and Daddy are to get to school and to work this morning, you will have to obey the traffic laws; you must stop at the stop signs and slow down in the congested areas. If you don't, you may still get there, but you may find it chaotic and nerve-wracking."

I further explained to her that while she and her Daddy were free to go to school and to work, others were also free to do the same. But, that freedom doesn't mean that *all free people* can go through the intersection *at the same time*!

Without rules at meetings, and those rules applying to everyone equally, the meetings often become something like a congested area of traffic; they turn into shouting matches, are run dictatorially with an unqualified person directing, or end up with few reaching their desired destination.

It is a fact of life that almost every human being will attend a meeting of some kind during his lifetime. If there is no communication at that meeting, there is no productivity, unless, of course, there is a political boss, a dictator, who tells the group what to do, when to do it, and how it must be done.

WHEN NO ONE, EXCEPT THE CHOSEN FEW, IS ALLOWED TO SPEAK, THERE IS OPPRESSION; WHEN EVERYONE FEELS THAT FREEDOM IS THE FREEDOM TO DO AS ONE PLEASES, THERE IS CHAOS.

Parliamentary law (parliamentary procedure), therefore, is the art of procedural rules that can enable a group of individuals in a free society, whether there are three or 3,000, to meet together and accomplish the purpose for which it has assembled.

No Skills Needed?

There may be so little knowledge of parliamentary procedure that one isn't even aware of his or her ignorance of the subject—I shall give an example. Recently, an educator who has a Ph.D. degree sent me a parliamentary procedure lesson plan to review for him. (Incidentally, I congratulate his group for finally realizing that parliamentary procedure is a must if our freedoms are to continue. They realize that today's youth is asking to participate, and that the only way participation can be successful is through the orderly process of using accepted rules of procedure. It is my belief that if these rules had been a part of our school curriculum; that is, if we had been taught how to participate, as well as how to listen, we would never have had the "hot summers" of the 60s.)

The lesson plan was written for teachers to use in teaching their students. Remember, however, most teachers did not learn this in school either. The first page had the comment: NO SKILLS WILL BE NEEDED BEFORE TEACHING THIS UNIT, AND NO EQUIPMENT WILL BE NECESSARY. Yet I have spent 26 years trying to simplify visual aids and materials so that my students and associates may be more aware of the importance of the rules. I can't imagine teachers being advised, however, that they need not have skills and equipment when teaching anything.

Perhaps the best example of how few educators are ever taught parliamentary procedure is explained in an article in the April 1971 issue of the *Parliamentary Journal*, the official magazine of the American Institute of Parliamentarians. The article was written by John Sullivan, Ph.D., of the University of Virginia. Dr. Sullivan served as parliamentarian in 1969–1970 for the University of Virginia Faculty of Arts and Sciences, a group with a membership of 450. Dr. Sullivan tells of the "chaotic sessions" involving the discussion of curriculum reform, the nature, function, role, and place of an ROTC program in a university, and student representation in faculty deliberations.

"If any faculty should have been expected to heed Mr. (Thomas) Jefferson's injunction concerning the importance of adhering to parliamentary laws it should have been Virginia," Dr. Sullivan writes, "yet, despite his advice, until the fall of 1969 the faculty of Arts and Sciences, the University's largest, most active and democratic, has assiduously avoided recourse to parliamentary form. . . . It was doubtful." he writes, "that anyone could be found who knew all the intricacies of Robert . . . still even simple matters like alternating speakers for and against a motion had to be explained without offending those who had never bothered to follow the rules . . . . Those unfamiliar with the manual at best came away confused and suspicious. Too often they saw parliamentary procedure as a way to accomplish their specific purpose rather than as a safeguard for the rights of the society and as a method of assuring full, free, and fair debate."

How many elementary schools, high schools, colleges, universities, and graduate schools had these 450 University of Virginia faculty members attended? Yet, from this article, it is apparent that almost none had ever taken a simple course in parliamentary procedure or anything else that had made them aware of the democratic process. Many of these faculty members had Ph.D. degrees, and the Arts and Science Division also includes the College of Law faculty.

Lack of Relevancy in Our Educational Systems—Three Examples

It is most unfortunate that our educational systems do not prepare their graduates for the positions they will hold in the public and private sectors of our society. This lack of relevancy shows itself quite often and in many glaring ways. Three immediate examples come to mind.

A close relative attended one of the better prep schools in the nation; he graduated from a private church-affiliated university; he graduated from a state university medical school; he interned for a year at a private university hospital. He spent a quarter of a century attending educational institutions. Yet, he was never *required* to take a course in public speaking and he was never *offered* a course in parliamentary procedure. Within a year after going into medical practice he was elected to the board of directors of a local service club and became vice-president of the Audubon Society. This man was totally unprepared for active leadership in his official capacity.

An attorney spent eight years attending a local university; four years in the College of Business and four years in the College of Law. He advised me that he was never taught parliamentary procedure, nor did the subject come up in classrooms.

A student who is now attending the College of Law has studied parliamentary procedure with me for several years. He wanted to convince the college to offer at least a short course in the subject. After completing his course in corporate law, with no mention made of procedure to be

5

used at corporate meetings, he asked the professor when the students would be offered a course. The professor looked at him quizzically, and then replied, "Oh, you can pick that up anywhere."

But, it *cannot* be picked up anywhere. It must be taught, practiced and accepted as a living part of our democratic principles and processes.

Lack of Leadership

The three previous examples indicate the apparent lack of knowledge demonstrated by both the educational and legal professions. But, it also effects our daily lives through the lack of leadership in our country.

In 1801 Thomas Jefferson wrote the first parliamentary authority that the young United States ever had, the *Jefferson's Manual.* In his manual he wrote, " ... No one is to disturb another in his speech by hissing, coughing or spitting ...."

In August of 1974, after years of weekly "shouting matches," a particular City Council passed a resolution that reads in part: "Conduct of the individual members during meetings of the Council is expected to reflect a total sense of respect for the offices held by those assembled to conduct business. Members shall be courteous to one another ...."

Both of the above, written 173 years apart, imply that orderly meetings were not then, nor are they now, the orders of the day. Yet, both bodies were elected by the people and it is assumed that those best qualified were elected.

The above-mentioned City Council includes three attorneys who were elected and several city attorneys who are available for consultation and who serve as parliamentarians for the Council. During one of the Council's infamous meetings, and after one of the local city attorneys had offered some erroneous parliamentary advice, I approached the attorneys to inquire about their parliamentary authority which was alleged to have been

Robert's Rules of Order. One of the attorneys admitted that he didn't know anything about parliamentary procedure, "and furthermore," he said, "I don't want to know anything about it."

What is important here is that *any* City Council effects our lives—all of our lives. The behavior of our leaders in sessions effects the decisions they make. If the leaders cannot be heard, you cannot be heard. PARLIAMENTARY PROCEDURE IS SYNONYMOUS WITH LEADERSHIP.

Political Conventions—Examples of How *Not* to Proceed

Perhaps the best example I can offer to illustrate the absolute need for an education in parliamentary procedures is your own television set. Every four years our political conventions are televised with their complementary chaos and confusion. I refer you to those events. The spectacle that you view is not unlike other political gatherings.

In 1973 I was asked to serve as parliamentarian for the National Women's Political Caucus at Houston. I requested a copy of their plans and/or standing rules to find out whether they were using *Jefferson's Manual, Robert's Rules of Order* or some other parliamentary authority. I needed to know in advance if their authority was in conflict with any of their rules in order to advise them accordingly.

I received a two-page document that included the names and activities of the rules committee. Robert's 555-page parliamentary authority had been reduced to less than one page of actual rules. The name of one of our Congresswomen, who is also a lawyer, headed the list of committee members.

I arrived in Houston the day before, and spent many hours trying to convince enough of the leaders that the Caucus must adopt a parliamentary authority, without which they would have no need for a parliamentarian because our role is only to advise them of said authority. I suggested to them that without rules there would be no

9

way 1,000 people could accomplish anything.

At the request of one of the leaders, I prepared a substitute for the committee report. The substitute included *Robert's* as the parliamentary authority. It was presented to the Caucus by the vice-chairman, who was also a member of the rules committee. The substitute motion was vehemently opposed. After two hours and 40 minutes of debate, it was finally adopted. The choices that this large group had were to proceed with a set of rules that could guarantee the rights of the members of the Caucus, and, as a result, assure full, free, and fair debate, or the otherwise inevitable—a series of shouting matches.

Many of the women in this group were legislators, congresswomen, judges and school teachers—a well-educated group. A woman who sat beside me at one of the meetings was a Congresswoman and a lawyer. She, too, made several offhand remarks about "getting bogged down in parliamentary procedure." This woman was a member of the Judicial Committee that was contemplating the impeachment of former President Nixon because he did not follow rules. I subsequently heard a speech on television in which the speaker related this woman's acute awareness of the lack of freedoms in our society. But, that is what parliamentary procedure is all about—the preservation of these freedoms.

Parliamentary Procedure Is a Fact of Life

I constantly run into disinclination to use parliamentary procedure at meetings. I submit to you, however, that whether or not groups want to use it, they are, in fact, using parliamentary rules the minute the meeting begins. It can be lousy procedure—and usually is—but, it *is* parliamentary procedure.

To illustrate that the use of parliamentary procedure is a fact of life, I shall remind you of when you first started using it. How about at the age of two or three? One youngster may have suggested, "Let's play ball." Didn't he or she just introduce an idea to the group? (The group may have consisted of two children.) In parliamentary terminology this is called a MAIN MOTION (an implied MAIN MOTION, right?).

If everyone is silent, the MAIN MOTION dies for lack of a SECOND. If, however, a second child says, "Yeh, let's do it," then there is an implied SECOND to the MAIN MOTION. Unless there are two people interested in an idea, there is little value in taking the time of the assembly to debate it, thus the reason for the SECOND.

Even at the age of four, you probably had a mind of your own and, no doubt, expressed yourself. This is referred to as the DISCUSSION or DEBATE, which follows the MAIN MOTION. If the DEBATE among a lively group of youngsters gets out of hand, then the CHAIRMAN, otherwise referred to as the mother, father, maid, teacher, or sitter, may have to step in and REFEREE or MODERATE the SESSION. If, however, the children *all*

11

start playing ball, the MAIN MOTION is adopted by a UNANIMOUS VOTE. If *most* of them start playing, then it is adopted by a MAJORITY VOTE.

Perhaps, during the DEBATE, one child says, "I'd like to play something, but I don't like to play ball, I'd rather play hide-and-seek." This child wants to AMEND the MAIN MOTION by striking the word "ball" and inserting in its place the words "hide-and-seek."

If, however, the youngsters become disinterested in the idea and start doing something else, the MAIN MOTION has failed.

Logic should prevail when studying any subject and Parliamentary Procedure is no exception. If the rules are not logical and practical, then they will not be used. My approach is very simple: THE RIGHTS OF THE MINORITY (that is you) SHOULD BE PROTECTED, BUT THE MAJORITY SHOULD RULE. THESE GOALS SHOULD BE ACCOMPLISHED IN AN ORDERLY, PRODUCTIVE MANNER: THUS THE NEED FOR RULES OF ORDER.

A New Era?

During the past couple of years, however, I have found that the words "parliamentary procedure," in my home area, are no longer solely synonymous with Lucille Place. There are others who are now saying the words freely, and some who are even applying the principles of the democratic process.

While attending a Regional conference of the American Institute of Parliamentarians in October 1975, I picked up a copy of the *Houston Chronicle* and the following headline caught my eye: "WOMAN MAYOR CALMING POLITICS IN SAN ANTONIO." I read the article thinking of the numerous "shouting matches" in our Councils, County Courts, school board meetings, and in our state legislative sessions. I wanted to learn her secret.

As I read the first few lines, I realized that after all these years I had finally lived to read where a politician was recognizing, and admitting, that the knowledge of parliamentary procedures could tame politics. The article reads in part: "My knowledge and use of *Robert's Rules of Order,* rather than my being a woman is, in my opinion, what has helped quiet down city council meetings."

I could hardly wait to talk to Mayor Lila Cockrell. During the telephone interview she advised me that she presides at the council meetings; and even though she has knowledge of parliamentary rules, she was not as effective when she was a member as she is now that she is the presiding officer. She also agreed that the use of rules of procedure is necessary for effective leadership.

Several years ago a member of the Memphis City

Council took one of my courses in parliamentary procedure and said that if he ever became the chairman he would have all council members take the course too.

Progress is being made in Memphis, but it is slow and still is not coming from the educational institutions that normally turn out the "leaders."

In the fall of 1974 Mrs. Jeanette Gunter, the coordinator of Community Services at the new Shelby State (Tennessee) Community College, phoned and asked me to teach a course in bridge. I agreed, and asked her why the college didn't offer a course in parliamentary procedure. She wasn't aware that I taught the subject, but was very excited about the possibilities. I started my first classes in January 1975. I have now taught three different sessions, two courses each, and plan to continue on a regular basis. I have also been asked to lead a workshop for the faculty. This community college is still the only educational institution that I find in this part of the country that offers such a course.

During the summer of 1974, at the request of a teacher who had been assigned to write a new unit on Freedom for the English Department of the Memphis City School System, I wrote a 16-page unit on parliamentary procedure. She had attended one of my workshops, after which she said she decided there could be no freedom without knowledge of parliamentary law. My only concern now is whether the unit will be taught.

The most encouragement I have seen, however, comes from a group of students at Memphis State University. For the past three years I have taught a one-day workshop sponsored by the Student Government Association at Memphis State. The workshops have had some degree of success, due largely to the enthusiasm of Dean of Students Emily Beck Weathers. She has placed a great deal of importance on the use of rules of procedure for the orderly and serious conduct of the Student Senate meetings.

Dave Lillard, the 1975 Speaker of the Senate, has also given much inspiration through his use of proper procedural rules. His expertise and enthusiasm, plus his desire not only to improve himself but to allow others to step into his role and learn as he has done, have created much interest among the students at the University.

During the recent fall session of 1975, one of the Senators, Dennis Harkness, introduced a bill recommending that the University offer a course in parliamentary procedure as a regular course in the college curriculum. As this book goes to press, the bill is in the Education Committee.

For the past two years I have taught a two-hour session for Dean Clarence Hampton in his leadership course at Memphis State. Some of the Student Government Association members also attend these classes.

On November 13, 1975, the Senate invited the faculty and friends to attend the Senate session. For the second time during my many years of interest in parliamentary procedure, I observed a truly professional meeting of an assembly. (The only other occasion was the 1975 Convention of the American Institute of Parliamentarians, which was presided over by the President, Darwin Patnode, Ph.D.) Dave Lillard and Darwin Patnode, both young men, presided impeccably, and there was free and full debate using the principles set forth by Thomas Jefferson and all parliamentarians who have followed.

This meeting of the Senate was Dean Weathers' farewell to the University and as she left she commented, "These students have started a movement that cannot be stopped." I agree!

15

Simplicity Is the Key to Communication

Assuming the assessment made by the Dean of Students at Memphis State University is a reality; that is, that the students have started a movement that cannot be stopped, parliamentary rules, then, must be written in a simple, practical, common-sense, and logical manner, so they can be understood. I shall proceed accordingly.

You Have Joined the Club

Let's assume you have just joined the City Civic Club (it could just as easily have been the neighborhood garden club; a high school or college organization; or a city, county, state or national governmental body). The reason you joined is clear: you think it is about time you became involved, and that you have something you believe you can offer. You are reading this book because, if you're going to spend your time on this project, you want to be assured of enough knowledge so that you can be effective.

You attended your first meeting today and found that others present were like yourself; they, too, had something to say. The problem you found, however, was that everyone wanted to say it at the same time. The chairman, whom you had always considered to be one of the knowledgeable leaders in the community, didn't know how to conduct the meeting; and many others present, whom you had also considered to be knowledgeable individuals, didn't know how to participate intelligently. The meeting turned out to be chaos and nothing was accomplished. No, I wasn't at *that* meeting, but I've attended before.

If you are over 40, let me take you back a few years— to the time when you, and most of the other citizens in your city, were sitting back and allowing someone else to run the show. You did little more than your share of complaining about what was going on. Our aforementioned "leaders" could handle the meetings in those days because the few who did attend didn't really care who presided, what they did, or how they did it. And when a disgruntled member showed up once in a while, his (or her) comments could always be nullified by labeling him a "trouble-maker."

But, let's talk about today! Perhaps a decade ago, what with the Vietnam conflict and the civil rights movement, many of the "followers" became disgruntled. They began to wonder if their "leaders" were really leading, or if they were just concerned about their own powerful and prestigious roles within the community. Or was it just ignorance?

Since so few educational institutions have ever taught the process of communicating, it is entirely possible that most of the problems of the world have been simply a breakdown in communications.

Obviously, then, if you want to continue your activities in the City Civic Club, you must do one of three things: 1) learn how to shout louder than anyone else; 2) learn rules by which orderly, thus productive, meetings can be possible; or 3) resign if you can't afford therapy sessions.

Let's assume, then, that you decided to learn the rules; otherwise you wouldn't be reading this book.

The balance of the book will deal with how your meeting today could have been orderly, productive, and democratic.

Twenty-four Situations

Below are 24 situations that I have found cover almost anything that may take place at a meeting. As you read them, ask yourself if they could logically occur at any meeting you may attend. I am assuming, of course, that you want to participate actively and that you (and others) are doing your own thinking.

Suppose you attend another meeting today and:

1. You want to bring a new idea before the group—what would you do. (See page 103.)
2. You do not want an idea, just introduced by another member, discussed at all—what would you do? (See page 103.)
3. You want to change some of the wording in an idea that is being discussed—what would you do? (See page 104.)
4. You want more study and investigation given the idea that is being discussed—what would you do? (See page 105.)
5. You want more time to study the subject; you may want to suggest another day, or even a particular hour, to bring it back for discussion—what would you do? (See page 106.)
6. You are tired of listening to so much discussion; or you may want to suggest a limit to the discussion—what would you do (See page 107.)
7. You want to forget about the idea for a while, but you *may* want it brought back for discussion at a later time—what would you do? (See page 109.)
8. You want a short break, or maybe even a long break—

what would you do? (See page 111.)

9. You want the meeting to end—what would you do? (See page 111.)

10. You realize the club's business cannot be completed within the absolute time limit for this meeting, yet there are things that must be done before next month's meeting—what would you do? (See page 112.)

11. A vote was just taken, but you weren't sure about the results of the vote. The presiding officer announced that the motion was adopted, but you thought you heard more "no" votes than "yes" votes—what would you do? (See page 113.)

12. You just offered an idea to the group and it is being discussed, yet you wish you hadn't—what would you do? (See page 114.)

13. a. At the beginning of the meeting the group decided which subjects they wanted to bring up first, but the chairman isn't following this procedure—what would you do? (See page 115.)

   b. Suppose, however, it has become apparent to you that item #3, under new business, should be considered before item #1—what would you do? (See page 116.)

14. a. The meeting has become so noisy you can't hear (or you are too hot or too cold); unless something is done you might as well go home because you are not getting anything out of the meeting—what would you do? (See page 116.)

   b. You are confused about the procedures that are being used and you want some clarification—what would you do? (See page 117.)

   c. The chairman just made a ruling and you don't agree with the ruling—what would you do? (See page 117.)

15. Someone brings up the idea of buying the past president a gift and suggests the club pay $500 for it. You don't want to spend more than $1.50; some of the other members are discussing other amounts. The

shouting began 30 minutes ago and they are still unde-
cided about the amount—what would you do? (See
page 118.)

16. a. Something was voted on earlier in this meeting but
you have now changed your mind about your
vote—what would you do? (See page 120.)
b. The meeting adjourned before you changed your
mind—what would you do? (See page 120.)

17. You want to present a cleanup project to your club, but
your proposal has at least three different parts to it
and you may not get recognition from the chairman
three different times to present all of them (remember, there are others at your meeting who want to participate too)—what would you do? (See page 122.)

18. Another member has just made a similar proposal;
that is, with several different parts to it, and you like
some of them but do not like others—what would you
do? (See page 123.)

19. A member has just brought up a motion concerning
recreation for your group. You agree that recreation
is in order, but you don't agree with many of the details presented by this member. You want to change
several of the words or phrases in the proposal. It appears, however, that too much time would be spent in
changing all of the words you propose to change.
What would you do? (See page 123.)

20. You are going to propose a matter that is controversial
and you feel sure some of the members will try to stop
the discussion, as well as use other maneuvers to kill it,
before it can be fully explained and debated. You are
convinced, however, that it is of such importance to
the community that a full and complete hearing
should be given the proposal before it is actually considered by final vote. What would you do? (See page
125.)

During my 26 years of interest in common parliamentary law, I have found that the answers to these situations are all that is needed, at even the most spirited meetings, to accomplish the goals of the organization and to assure safeguards for the rights of the society; and with methods by which full, free, and fair debate may be attained. If your organization becomes more technical, I suggest you consult *Robert's Rules of Order, Newly Revised.* Regardless of which parliamentary authority you use, they are all based on common parliamentary law, without which there can be little or no order.

THE ABSENCE OF ORDER AT A MEETING CAN ASSURE THE ABSENCE OF PRODUCTIVITY; AND WHEN FREEDOM OF SPEECH BECOMES THE FREEDOM FOR EVERYONE TO SPEAK AT THE SAME TIME, THEN FREEDOM IS INEVITABLY LOST.

Part II

THE NEED FOR RULES OF ORDER: THE *MOTIONS CHART*

Introducing the Motions Chart

Before presenting and explaining the answers to my questions, I must first give practical examples of the need for rules of order and why we refer to them. By specific illustrations, you will recognize their functional value.

Following are three pictures of the MOTIONS CHART that I have used for many years in teaching my classes. I have found the motions on the front of the chart and the information on the back to be almost all that is needed to conduct, or participate in, any orderly, productive, democratic meeting.

I have been advised by other instructors and parliamentarians to add more information to this chart. I find, however, that I have been successful because I don't load my students' minds with too many facts. I prefer giving them the *essentials* that they can easily learn—rather than giving them too much and having their minds so cluttered that they end up learning nothing.

ADJOURN

RECESS

TABLE

CLOSE DEBATE

LIMIT DEBATE

POSTPONE DEFINITELY

REFER TO COMMITTEE

AMEND AMENDMENT

AMEND

POSTPONE INDEFINITELY

MAIN MOTION

SEE REVERSE SIDE

DEFINITIONS:

"S" means the motion must be seconded.

"D" means it may be debated.

"A" means it may be amended.

"M" requires a majority vote to pass.

"2" means it takes a 2/3 vote to pass.

"R" after the motion has been voted on, it may be reconsidered.

DESIGN SERVICES OF MEMPHIS • 1702 Lawrence Pl. • Memphis, Tn. 38112 • Phone 901 / 278-6739

PRINTED IN U S A

25

PARLIAMENTARY PROCEDURE
MOTIONS CHART

Lucille Place, CPP
Richard S. Kain, CPP

Motion	S	D	A	M / 2	R
ADJOURN	S			M	
RECESS	S		A	M	
TABLE	S			M	
CLOSE DEBATE	S			2	R
LIMIT DEBATE	S		A	2	R
POSTPONE DEFINITELY	S	D	A	M	R
REFER TO COMMITTEE	S	D	A	M	R
AMEND AMENDMENT	S	D		M	R
AMEND	S	D	A	M	R
POSTPONE INDEFINITELY	S	D		M	R
MAIN MOTION	S	D	A	M	R

SEE REVERSE SIDE

DEFINITIONS:

"S" means the motion must be seconded.

"D" means it may be debated.

"A" means it may be amended.

"M" requires a majority vote to pass.

"2" means it takes a 2/3 vote to pass.

"R" after the motion has been voted on, it may be reconsidered.

DESIGN SERVICES OF MEMPHIS · 1702 Lawrence Pl. · Memphis, Tn. 38112 · Phone 901 / 278-6739

USE OF THE CHART:

1. Consider the chart as a ladder with MAIN MOTION as the bottom rung.
2. Motions are MADE GOING UP the ladder and VOTED ON GOING DOWN the ladder.
3. As motions are MADE the SLIDES ARE PUSHED TO THE LEFT.
4. As motions are VOTED on the slides are PUSHED BACK TO THE RIGHT.
5. Motions lower on the ladder than the last one made are out of order.

Example:

Push all slides to the right. This means all SDAM2R's are covered. When a main motion is made, seconded and stated by the chair, pull that slide to the left. This is the pending motion and you are now able to see that the motion must be seconded (S); may be debated (D); may be amended (A); takes a majority vote to pass (M); and may be reconsidered after the vote is taken (R).

At this point any or all of the motions on the ladder may be added to this MAIN MOTION, assuming, of course, they are made going up the ladder. If however, the next motion after the MAIN MOTION is to postpone to the next month's meeting (POSTPONE DEFINITELY) and after this motion has been seconded and stated by the chair (slide is then pulled to the left), the next motion is to refer the MAIN MOTION to a committee, the motion to REFER is out of order because it is lower on the ladder.

OTHER PARLIAMENTARY MANEUVERS COMMONLY USED:

"DIVISION" — When there is doubt about the vote on a motion and you want another vote taken, just call out "Division." This is a demand that a standing vote be taken.

"POINT OF INFORMATION" — If you need information concerning something relevant to business on the floor, a question about parliamentary procedure, etc., just call out, "Point of information, Mister Chairman." The chairman will ask you to state your point and act accordingly.

"POINT OF ORDER" — If things seem to be completely out of hand, which occurs too frequently, just call out, "Point of order, Madam Chairman." Again, you are asked to state your point.

"I have used this motion chart (on a larger scale) with my classes for many years. I have found that using it allows my students to preside with confidence or participate intelligently at any meeting."

Lucille Plese

Certified Professional Parliamentarian.
Chairman Accrediting Committee (1975) American Institute of Parliamentarians.
Member Commission on American Parliamentary Procedure

27

The chart shown on page 29 indicates that a member has just made a MAIN MOTION(put an idea on the floor). The motion has been SECONDED, then STATED by the presiding officer, after which the MOTION has become the PROPERTY OF THE ASSEMBLY and no longer belongs to the person who made the motion. No member need ever ask the maker of the motion for his/her permission to do anything to the motion, simply because the motion no longer belongs to him/her It belongs to the organization.

The MAIN MOTION slide has been pulled to the left and you can readily see that the main motion *must* be seconded (S); *may* be debated (D); *may* be amended (A); *requires* a majority vote to adopt (M); and *may* be reconsidered after the vote is taken (R).

Since the language of the parliamentary procedure is language that you do not normally use, you must *learn* this language. For that reason, I am giving you the exact words to be used during these procedures. I suggest you repeat these words and phrases until they become a part of your normal vocabulary. If you do not, you will find yourself reaching for words that will not come without hesitation; and when you hesitate, you have lost some of your leadership influence. It's that simple!

MAIN MOTION DRILL

Member A: "Mr. Chairman."

Chairman: "The chair recognizes Mr. A.

Member A: "Mr. Chairman, I move that we have a picnic."

Chairman: "Is there a second to this motion?"

Member B: "I second the motion." (Any number of

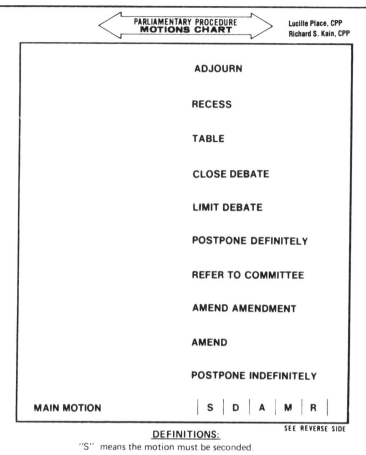

PARLIAMENTARY PROCEDURE
MOTIONS CHART

Lucille Place, CPP
Richard S. Kain, CPP

ADJOURN

RECESS

TABLE

CLOSE DEBATE

LIMIT DEBATE

POSTPONE DEFINITELY

REFER TO COMMITTEE

AMEND AMENDMENT

AMEND

POSTPONE INDEFINITELY

MAIN MOTION | S | D | A | M | R |

SEE REVERSE SIDE

DEFINITIONS:

"S" means the motion must be seconded.
"D" means it may be debated.
"A" means it may be amended.
"M" requires a majority vote to pass.
"2" means it takes a 2/3 vote to pass.
"R" after the motion has been voted on, it may be reconsidered.

DESIGN SERVICES OF MEMPHIS • 1702 Lawrence Pl. • Memphis, Tn. 38112 • Phone 901 / 278-6739

29

members may call out, "I second the motion" or just "Second." The member [s] does not have to be recognized by the chair in order to second the motion. This, then, is the logical reason for not requiring the name of the person, or persons, who seconded a motion to be included in the minutes[record] of the meeting. It may be difficult for the secretary to determine who first seconded the motion, and surely you don't want to waste the time trying to determine whose name should go into the minutes.)

Chairman: "A motion has been made and seconded that we have a picnic. Is there any discussion (debate)? The motion is debatable (D), may be amended (A), requires only a majority (M) vote to pass (adopt), and may be reconsidered (R) after the vote is taken."

Since the maker of the motion has first priority to debate the motion, the chairman then may ask, "Does the maker of the motion wish to debate the motion?"

When it is apparent that the debate is over, that is, no one is asking to be recognized, the next obvious step is to bring the motion to an immediate vote, right? Is there any logical reason for the presiding officer to ask, "Are you ready for the question?" Not unless you are prepared for all of the members present to respond with either a "yes" or a "no."

Several years ago I served as the sergeant-at-arms at a convention where 5,000 assembled in Washington, D.C. As usual, almost no one present, including the presiding officer, knew anything about rules that could assure some degree of order, and there was enough confusion without everyone being asked to respond to such a nonsensical question. If there is a motion on the floor and no one is asking to debate it, then it must be disposed of; and how else do you dispose of a motion other than by asking the members present whether they approve or disapprove of it (bringing it to a vote)?

Since there were no amendments or other motions attached to this main motion, the presiding officer will merely say, "Hearing no further debate, all in favor say 'aye' [pause for vote]; all opposed say, 'no' [pause for vote]"; after which the chairman announces the results: "The motion is adopted" or "The motion fails."

MAIN MOTION with AMENDMENT DRILL

Let's assume there is a main motion on the floor that reads: "That we have a picnic and dance." During the debate (discussion) a member wants to change some of the wording in the main motion. This can be done by AMENDING the main motion.

Amendments can be made in only three ways:

1. A word (or words) can be ADDED.
2. A word (or words) can be STRUCK OUT (deleted).
3. A word (or words) can be STRUCK OUT and a word (or words) INSERTED in its (their) place (by STRIKING OUT and INSERTING).

ADDING: "I move that we amend the main motion by adding the words 'at Overton Park.'"

STRIKING: "I move that we amend the main motion by striking the word 'dance.'"

STRIKING AND INSERTING: "I move that we amend the main motion by striking the word 'picnic' and inserting in its place the word 'dinner.'"

The chairman states: "Is there a second?" (Pause for the second. If none is made, the chairman announces, "The motion dies for lack of a second.")

Chairman's responses to the above motions (after the motion has been seconded):

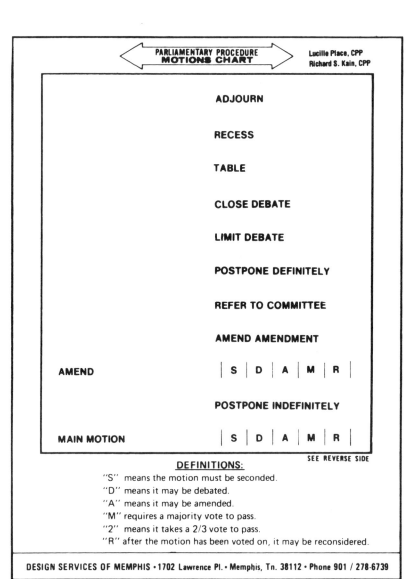

PARLIAMENTARY PROCEDURE
MOTIONS CHART

Lucille Place, CPP
Richard S. Kain, CPP

ADJOURN

RECESS

TABLE

CLOSE DEBATE

LIMIT DEBATE

POSTPONE DEFINITELY

REFER TO COMMITTEE

AMEND AMENDMENT

AMEND | S | D | A | M | R |

POSTPONE INDEFINITELY

MAIN MOTION | S | D | A | M | R |

SEE REVERSE SIDE

DEFINITIONS:

"S" means the motion must be seconded.

"D" means it may be debated.

"A" means it may be amended.

"M" requires a majority vote to pass.

"2" means it takes a 2/3 vote to pass.

"R" after the motion has been voted on, it may be reconsidered.

DESIGN SERVICES OF MEMPHIS • 1702 Lawrence Pl. • Memphis, Tn. 38112 • Phone 901 / 278-6739

PRINTED IN U S A

33

ADDING EXAMPLE:

Chairman: "A motion has been made and seconded that the main motion be amended by adding the words 'at Overton Park.' Is there any discussion? The debate is on the amendment only."

STRIKING OUT EXAMPLE:

Chairman: "A motion has been made and seconded that the main motion be amended by striking the word 'dance.' Is there any discussion? The discussion at this time is on the amendment only." . . ."Is there further debate?"

STRIKING OUT and INSERTING EXAMPLE:

Chairman: "A motion has been made and seconded that the main motion be amended by striking the word 'picnic' and inserting in its place the word 'dinner.' Is there any discussion?" . . ."Is there further debate?" "Hearing none, we will now vote. We are voting on the amendment only. All in favor of the amendment, which is to strike the word 'picnic' and insert the word 'dinner,' say 'aye.' Those opposed say 'no.' (Pause for each vote.). . . . The motion is adopted."

Push the AMEND slide back to the right. The board now has only the MAIN MOTION slide to the left, representing the main motion that has been amended. You are aware that the amendment has been disposed of—it was voted on—thus the IMEDIATELY PENDING MOTION (QUESTION) is the main motion in the form to which it was amended.

The main motion is now brought to a vote and, let's assume, the main motion was adopted. How would the chart look now?

ADJOURN

RECESS

TABLE

CLOSE DEBATE

LIMIT DEBATE

POSTPONE DEFINITELY

REFER TO COMMITTEE

AMEND AMENDMENT

AMEND

POSTPONE INDEFINITELY

| MAIN MOTION | S | D | A | M | R |

SEE REVERSE SIDE

DEFINITIONS:

"S" means the motion must be seconded.

"D" means it may be debated.

"A" means it may be amended.

"M" requires a majority vote to pass.

"2" means it takes a 2/3 vote to pass.

"R" after the motion has been voted on, it may be reconsidered.

DESIGN SERVICES OF MEMPHIS • 1702 Lawrence Pl. • Memphis, Tn. 38112 • Phone 901 / 278-6739

PRINTED IN U.S.A.

All slides are moved to the right which indicates that there is no business pending.

Chairman: "Is there any further business to come before this assembly?"

Member C: "Mr. Chairman."

Chairman: "The Chair recognizes Member C."

Member C: "Mr. Chairman, I move that the club purchase a clubhouse.

Chairman: "Is there a second?"

Member M: "I second the motion."

Chairman: "A motion has been made and seconded that the club purchase a clubhouse. Is there any discussion (debate)? Does the maker of the motion wish to debate the motion?"

ADJOURN

RECESS

TABLE

CLOSE DEBATE

LIMIT DEBATE

POSTPONE DEFINITELY

REFER TO COMMITTEE

AMEND AMENDMENT

AMEND

POSTPONE INDEFINITELY

MAIN MOTION

SEE REVERSE SIDE

DEFINITIONS:

"S" means the motion must be seconded.
"D" means it may be debated.
"A" means it may be amended.
"M" requires a majority vote to pass.
"2" means it takes a 2/3 vote to pass.
"R" after the motion has been voted on, it may be reconsidered.

DESIGN SERVICES OF MEMPHIS • 1702 Lawrence Pl. • Memphis, Tn. 38112 • Phone 901 / 278-6739

PRINTED IN U.S.A.

37

The MAIN MOTION slide has been moved to the left side of the chart, which indicates that the immediately pending question is the main motion.

During the debate Member W wants to amend the main motion.

Member W: "Mr. Chairman."

Chairman: "The Chair recognizes Member W."

Member W: "I move that the main motion be amended by adding the words 'on the Mississippi River.' "

Chairman: "Is there a second?"

Member N: "I second the motion."

Chairman: "A motion has been made and seconded that the main motion be amended by adding the words 'on the Mississippi River.' Is there any debate? The debate now is on the amendment only. If the club desires to build a clubhouse, do you want it built on the Mississippi River? The debate cannot go into whether you want a clubhouse, but only whether you want it on the Mississippi River."

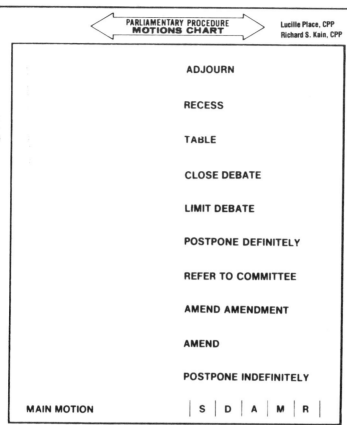

Lucille Place, CPP
Richard S. Kain, CPP

ADJOURN

RECESS

TABLE

CLOSE DEBATE

LIMIT DEBATE

POSTPONE DEFINITELY

REFER TO COMMITTEE

AMEND AMENDMENT

AMEND

POSTPONE INDEFINITELY

| MAIN MOTION | S | D | A | M | R |

SEE REVERSE SIDE

DEFINITIONS:

"S" means the motion must be seconded.
"D" means it may be debated.
"A" means it may be amended.
"M" requires a majority vote to pass.
"2" means it takes a 2/3 vote to pass.
"R" after the motion has been voted on, it may be reconsidered.

DESIGN SERVICES OF MEMPHIS • 1702 Lawrence Pl. • Memphis, Tn. 38112 • Phone 901 / 278-6739

The AMEND slide has been moved to the left of the CHART, which indicates that the immediately pending question is the amendment.

Chairman: "Is there further debate on the amendment?" . . . "Hearing none, we will now vote on the amendment, which is to add the words 'on the Mississippi River.' All in favor say 'aye.' . . . All opposed say 'no.' . . . The motion to amend is adopted."

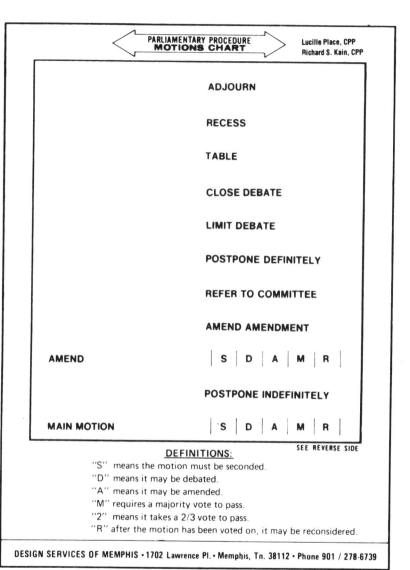

PARLIAMENTARY PROCEDURE
MOTIONS CHART

Lucille Place, CPP
Richard S. Kain, CPP

ADJOURN

RECESS

TABLE

CLOSE DEBATE

LIMIT DEBATE

POSTPONE DEFINITELY

REFER TO COMMITTEE

AMEND AMENDMENT

AMEND

| S | D | A | M | R |

POSTPONE INDEFINITELY

MAIN MOTION

| S | D | A | M | R |

SEE REVERSE SIDE

DEFINITIONS:

"S" means the motion must be seconded.
"D" means it may be debated.
"A" means it may be amended.
"M" requires a majority vote to pass.
"2" means it takes a 2/3 vote to pass.
"R" after the motion has been voted on, it may be reconsidered.

DESIGN SERVICES OF MEMPHIS • 1702 Lawrence Pl. • Memphis, Tn. 38112 • Phone 901 / 278-6739

PRINTED IN U.S.A

41

The AMEND slide has been moved back to the right of the CHART, which means that the immediately pending question is the amended main motion.

Chairman: "The immediately pending question now is the main motion as amended, which reads: 'That the club purchase a clubhouse . . . on the Mississippi River.' Is there any debate?" . . . "Is there further debate?" . . . Hearing none, we are ready to vote. All in favor say 'aye.' . . . Those opposed say 'no.' . . . The motion is adopted. The Chair appoints Members C, X, and Y as a committee to implement the motion."

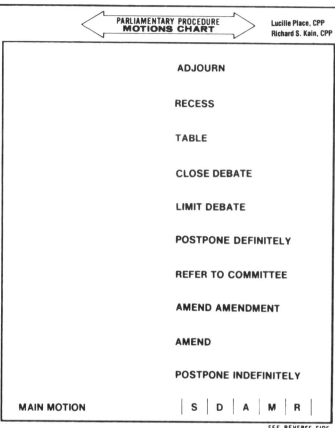

ADJOURN

RECESS

TABLE

CLOSE DEBATE

LIMIT DEBATE

POSTPONE DEFINITELY

REFER TO COMMITTEE

AMEND AMENDMENT

AMEND

POSTPONE INDEFINITELY

| MAIN MOTION | S | D | A | M | R |

SEE REVERSE SIDE

DEFINITIONS:

"S" means the motion must be seconded.
"D" means it may be debated.
"A" means it may be amended.
"M" requires a majority vote to pass.
"2" means it takes a 2/3 vote to pass.
"R" after the motion has been voted on, it may be reconsidered.

DESIGN SERVICES OF MEMPHIS • 1702 Lawrence Pl. • Memphis, Tn. 38112 • Phone 901 / 278-6739

PRINTED IN U.S.A

The MAIN MOTION slide has again been moved back to the right of the chart, which means that there is no business pending (nothing on the floor).

Chairman: "Is there further business to come before this assembly?"

Member T: "Mr. Chairman."

Chairman: "The Chair recognizes Member T."

Member T: "Mr. Chairman, I move that the club sponsor a spaghetti dinner."

Chairman: "Is there a second?"

Member Y: "I second the motion."

Chairman: "A motion has been made and seconded that the club sponsor a spaghetti dinner. Is there any debate?"

ADJOURN

RECESS

TABLE

CLOSE DEBATE

LIMIT DEBATE

POSTPONE DEFINITELY

REFER TO COMMITTEE

AMEND AMENDMENT

AMEND

POSTPONE INDEFINITELY

MAIN MOTION

SEE REVERSE SIDE

DEFINITIONS:

"S" means the motion must be seconded.
"D" means it may be debated.
"A" means it may be amended.
"M" requires a majority vote to pass.
"2" means it takes a 2/3 vote to pass.
"R" after the motion has been voted on, it may be reconsidered.

DESIGN SERVICES OF MEMPHIS • 1702 Lawrence Pl. • Memphis, Tn. 38112 • Phone 901 / 278-6739

PRINTED IN U.S.A.

The MAIN MOTION slide has been moved to the left side of the chart, which indicates that the immediately pending question is the main motion.

During the debate Member R wants to amend the motion.

Member R: "Mr. Chairman."

Chairman: "The Chair recognizes Member R."

Member R: "Mr. Chairman, I move that the main motion be amended by adding the words 'at the Italian Restaurant.'"

Several members call out, "I second the motion."

Chairman: "A motion has been made and seconded that the main motion be amended by adding the words 'at the Italian Restaurant.' Is there any debate?"

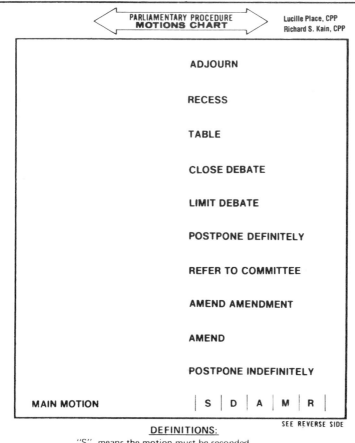

ADJOURN

RECESS

TABLE

CLOSE DEBATE

LIMIT DEBATE

POSTPONE DEFINITELY

REFER TO COMMITTEE

AMEND AMENDMENT

AMEND

POSTPONE INDEFINITELY

MAIN MOTION	S	D	A	M	R

SEE REVERSE SIDE

DEFINITIONS:

"S" means the motion must be seconded.

"D" means it may be debated.

"A" means it may be amended.

"M" requires a majority vote to pass.

"2" means it takes a 2/3 vote to pass.

"R" after the motion has been voted on, it may be reconsidered.

DESIGN SERVICES OF MEMPHIS • 1702 Lawrence Pl. • Memphis, Tn. 38112 • Phone 901 / 278-6739

PRINTED IN U.S.A

The AMEND slide has been moved to the left side of the chart, which indicates that the immediately pending question is the amendment (the motion on the floor is the amendment).

During the debate Member S wants to amend the amendment.

Member S: "Mr. Chairman."

Chairman: "The Chair recognizes Member S."

Member S: "Mr. Chairman, I move that the amendment be amended by adding the words 'and that the proceeds be used to defray some of the cost of the Mississippi River clubhouse.'"

Several members call out, "Second."

Chairman: "A motion has been made and seconded that the amendment be amended by adding the words 'and that the proceeds be used to defray some of the cost of the Mississippi River clubhouse.' Is there any debate? The debate now must be limited to the amendment to the amendment, which is not whether you want a spaghetti dinner or whether you want it at the Italian Restaurant, but whether you want the proceeds to be used on the Mississippi River clubhouse."

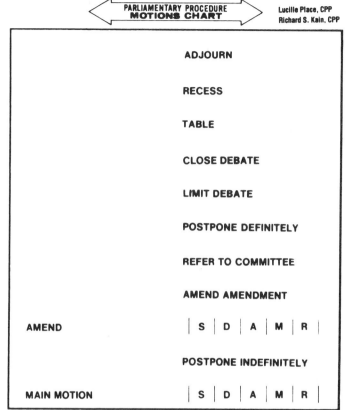

ADJOURN

RECESS

TABLE

CLOSE DEBATE

LIMIT DEBATE

POSTPONE DEFINITELY

REFER TO COMMITTEE

AMEND AMENDMENT

| AMEND | | S | D | A | M | R | |

POSTPONE INDEFINITELY

| MAIN MOTION | | S | D | A | M | R | |

SEE REVERSE SIDE

DEFINITIONS:

"S" means the motion must be seconded.
"D" means it may be debated.
"A" means it may be amended.
"M" requires a majority vote to pass.
"2" means it takes a 2/3 vote to pass.
"R" after the motion has been voted on, it may be reconsidered.

DESIGN SERVICES OF MEMPHIS • 1702 Lawrence Pl. • Memphis, Tn. 38112 • Phone 901 / 278-6739

PRINTED IN U S A

ADJOURN

RECESS

TABLE

CLOSE DEBATE

LIMIT DEBATE

POSTPONE DEFINITELY

REFER TO COMMITTEE

AMEND AMENDMENT	S	D		M	R
AMEND	S	D	A	M	R

POSTPONE INDEFINITELY

MAIN MOTION	S	D	A	M	R

SEE REVERSE SIDE

DEFINITIONS:

"S" means the motion must be seconded.
"D" means it may be debated.
"A" means it may be amended.
"M" requires a majority vote to pass.
"2" means it takes a 2/3 vote to pass.
"R" after the motion has been voted on, it may be reconsidered.

DESIGN SERVICES OF MEMPHIS • 1702 Lawrence Pl. • Memphis, Tn. 38112 • Phone 901 / 278-6739

PRINTED IN U S A

50

The AMEND AMENDMENT slide has been moved to the left side of the chart, which indicates that the immediately pending question is the amendment to the amendment.

The only way you can have order at a meeting and thus get something accomplished is that there be only one thing discussed at any one time. As you have observed, I refer to this as the IMMEDIATELY PENDING QUESTION. At this particular time there are three motions on the floor: the main motion, the amendment, and the amendment to the amendment. Unless a member makes a motion to CLOSE DEBATE, and this motion is adopted by a two-thirds vote, each of these three motions will continue to be debated, but they will be debated one at a time.

The motion that can be debated now is the amendment to amend; after this motion is voted on, whether it passes or fails, the next motion to be debated and voted on will be the motion to amend. After that motion is voted on, pass or fail, the next motion to be debated and voted on will be the main motion.

Chairman: "Is there further debate on the amendment to the amendment, which is . . .? . . . Hearing none, we will now vote. All in favor say 'aye.' . . . All opposed say 'no.' . . . The motion is adopted."

ADJOURN

RECESS

TABLE

CLOSE DEBATE

LIMIT DEBATE

POSTPONE DEFINITELY

REFER TO COMMITTEE

AMEND AMENDMENT

AMEND | S | D | A | M | R |

POSTPONE INDEFINITELY

MAIN MOTION | S | D | A | M | R |

SEE REVERSE SIDE

DEFINITIONS:

"S" means the motion must be seconded.

"D" means it may be debated.

"A" means it may be amended.

"M" requires a majority vote to pass.

"2" means it takes a 2/3 vote to pass.

"R" after the motion has been voted on, it may be reconsidered.

DESIGN SERVICES OF MEMPHIS • 1702 Lawrence Pl. • Memphis, Tn. 38112 • Phone 901 / 278-6739

PRINTED IN U.S.A.

52

The AMEND AMENDMENT slide has been moved back to the right side of the chart, which indicates that the immediately pending question now is the amendment.

Chairman: "The immediately pending question now is the amendment as has been amended, which reads: 'at the Italian Restaurant . . . and that the proceeds be used to defray some of the cost of the Mississippi River clubhouse.' Is there further debate? Your debate now is limited to the site of the Italian Restaurant *and* whether you agree with the proceeds going to the clubhouse project."

At this point in time, if a member wished to amend further, the AMEND AMENDMENT slide is still available.

Chairman: "Is there further debate? . . . Hearing none, we will now vote. All in favor say 'aye.' . . . All opposed say 'no.' . . . The motion is adopted."

Lucille Place, CPP
Richard S. Kain, CPP

ADJOURN

RECESS

TABLE

CLOSE DEBATE

LIMIT DEBATE

POSTPONE DEFINITELY

REFER TO COMMITTEE

AMEND AMENDMENT

AMEND

POSTPONE INDEFINITELY

MAIN MOTION | S | D | A | M | R |

SEE REVERSE SIDE

DEFINITIONS:

"S" means the motion must be seconded.

"D" means it may be debated.

"A" means it may be amended.

"M" requires a majority vote to pass.

"2" means it takes a 2/3 vote to pass.

"R" after the motion has been voted on, it may be reconsidered.

DESIGN SERVICES OF MEMPHIS • 1702 Lawrence Pl. • Memphis, Tn. 38112 • Phone 901 / 278-6739

PRINTED IN U.S.A

54

The AMEND slide has been moved to the right side of the CHART, which indicates that the immediately pending question now is the main motion as it has been amended twice.

Chairman: "The immediately pending question now is the main motion, which has been twice amended. The main motion now reads: 'That the club sponsor a spaghetti dinner . . . at the Italian Restaurant . . . and that the proceeds be used to defray some of the cost of the Mississippi River clubhouse.' Is there any further discussion? Any part of this may be debated at this time because it is all a part of the main motion now. . . . Is there further debate? . . . Hearing none, we will now vote. All in favor say 'aye.' . . . All opposed say 'no.' . . . The motion is adopted and the Chair appoints Members A, B, and T as a committee to expedite the motion. Is there further business to come before the assembly?"

The MAIN MOTION slide has been moved to the right side of the chart, which indicates that there is nothing on the floor (no pending question).

ADJOURN

RECESS

TABLE

CLOSE DEBATE

LIMIT DEBATE

POSTPONE DEFINITELY

REFER TO COMMITTEE

AMEND AMENDMENT

AMEND

POSTPONE INDEFINITELY

MAIN MOTION

SEE REVERSE SIDE

DEFINITIONS:

"S" means the motion must be seconded.
"D" means it may be debated.
"A" means it may be amended.
"M" requires a majority vote to pass.
"2" means it takes a 2/3 vote to pass.
"R" after the motion has been voted on, it may be reconsidered.

DESIGN SERVICES OF MEMPHIS • 1702 Lawrence Pl. • Memphis, Tn. 38112 • Phone 901 / 278-6739

PRINTED IN U.S.A

57

How to Determine When Motions Are Out of Order

Let's assume that the following motions have been made:
1. A main motion.
2. A motion to amend the main motion.
3. A motion to amend the amendment.
The chart would then look like this:

A motion could now be made to REFER TO COM-MITTEE; or to POSTPONE DEFINITELY (this means to a definite, or specific, period of time, that is, to "our next meeting," etc.); or to LIMIT DEBATE; or to CLOSE DEBATE (PREVIOUS QUESTION is used here, also, and is the more sophisticated terminology); or to TABLE (when tabling a motion, it means tabling the main motion and, of course, any other motion that is attached to it, such as an amendment, etc); or to RECESS; or to ADJOURN.

Lucille Place, CPP
Richard S. Kain, CPP

ADJOURN

RECESS

TABLE

CLOSE DEBATE

LIMIT DEBATE

POSTPONE DEFINITELY

REFER TO COMMITTEE

| AMEND AMENDMENT | S | D | | M | R |
| AMEND | S | D | A | M | R |

POSTPONE INDEFINITELY

| MAIN MOTION | S | D | A | M | R |

SEE REVERSE SIDE

DEFINITIONS:

"S" means the motion must be seconded.
"D" means it may be debated.
"A" means it may be amended.
"M" requires a majority vote to pass.
"2" means it takes a 2/3 vote to pass.
"R" after the motion has been voted on, it may be reconsidered.

DESIGN SERVICES OF MEMPHIS • 1702 Lawrence Pl. • Memphis, Tn. 38112 • Phone 901 / 278-6739

PRINTED IN U.S.A

59

Let's assume that Member L wants to postpone the whole matter until the next meeting of the organization. He would go through the procedure of getting recognized by the Chairman, after which he would make his motion to postpone definitely (until the next meeting.)

Now the chart looks like this:

But then Member D wants to make a motion to REFER TO COMMITTEE. After recognition by the chairman, she makes her motion to "Refer the question to a committee of three members, to be appointed by the chairman."

Chairman: "The motion to refer to a committee is out of order at this time. Is there further debate on the immediately pending question, which is to postpone to our next meeting?"

Is the Chairman Correct or is This the Chairman's Way of Assuring that the Meeting Remains Under His Control?

It is at this point during my workshops or classes that I am able to determine just how little my students, regardless of their educational background, know about rules of order. Until now they generally don't appear to be even aware that the title of the accepted parliamentary authority has RULES OF ORDER as a part. Seldom do I find even one person who can intelligently give me the answer. And, of course, unless the members attending the meeting know whether the chairman is correct, the chairman can do as he/she pleases, and many chairmen do just that!

ADJOURN

RECESS

TABLE

CLOSE DEBATE

LIMIT DEBATE

POSTPONE DEFINITELY | S | D | A | M | R |

REFER TO COMMiTTEE

AMEND AMENDMENT | S | D | | M | R |

AMEND | S | D | A | M | R |

POSTPONE INDEFINITELY

MAIN MOTION | S | D | A | M | R |

SEE REVERSE SIDE

DEFINITIONS:

''S'' means the motion must be seconded.
''D'' means it may be debated.
''A'' means it may be amended.
''M'' requires a majority vote to pass.
''2'' means it takes a 2/3 vote to pass.
''R'' after the motion has been voted on, it may be reconsidered.

DESIGN SERVICES OF MEMPHIS • 1702 Lawrence Pl. • Memphis, Tn. 38112 • Phone 901 / 278-6739

PRINTED IN U.S.A.

RULES OF ORDER means just what it says—there, is an order in which the motions can be made. Any motion that is made going up the "ladder" on the chart is in order; but when a motion is made coming down the chart, it is out of order.

EXAMPLE: If Member D had made a motion to limit debate, close debate, table, recess, or adjourn, the motion would have been in order because these motions are above the motion to postpone definitely. Since Member D made a motion that is down the ladder (lower in position), the motion was out of order. From any specific position, MOTIONS THAT ARE HIGHER ON THE LADDER HAVE PRECEDENCE OVER THE MOTIONS THAT ARE LOWER ON THE LADDER.

Let's further assume that the motion to postpone definitely was brought to a vote and it failed. Now the chart looks like this:

ADJOURN

RECESS

TABLE

CLOSE DEBATE

LIMIT DEBATE

POSTPONE DEFINITELY

REFER TO COMMITTEE

| AMEND AMENDMENT | S | D | | M | R |
| AMEND | S | D | A | M | R |

POSTPONE INDEFINITELY

| MAIN MOTION | S | D | A | M | R |

SEE REVERSE SIDE

DEFINITIONS:

"S" means the motion must be seconded.
"D" means it may be debated.
"A" means it may be amended.
"M" requires a majority vote to pass.
"2" means it takes a 2/3 vote to pass.
"R" after the motion has been voted on, it may be reconsidered.

DESIGN SERVICES OF MEMPHIS • 1702 Lawrence Pl. • Memphis, Tn. 38112 • Phone 901 / 278-6739

PRINTED IN U.S.A

Now, would the motion to REFER TO COMMIT-TEE be in order? Yes, because there are no motions on the floor that are higher in "rank" (higher on the ladder).

In the following illustration, I have pulled the MAIN MOTION, REFER TO COMMITTEE, POSTPONE DE-FINITELY, and RECESS slides to the left:

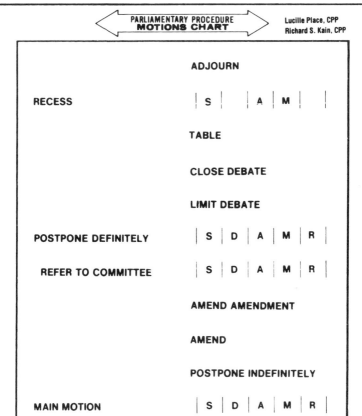

Lucille Place, CPP
Richard S. Kain, CPP

ADJOURN

RECESS | S | | A | M | |

TABLE

CLOSE DEBATE

LIMIT DEBATE

POSTPONE DEFINITELY | S | D | A | M | R |

REFER TO COMMITTEE | S | D | A | M | R |

AMEND AMENDMENT

AMEND

POSTPONE INDEFINITELY

MAIN MOTION | S | D | A | M | R |

SEE REVERSE SIDE

DEFINITIONS:

"S" means the motion must be seconded.
"D" means it may be debated.
"A" means it may be amended.
"M" requires a majority vote to pass.
"2" means it takes a 2/3 vote to pass.
"R" after the motion has been voted on, it may be reconsidered.

DESIGN SERVICES OF MEMPHIS • 1702 Lawrence Pl. • Memphis, Tn. 38112 • Phone 901 / 278-6739

PRINTED IN U S A

65

The motions refer to committee, postpone definitely, and recess also have an "A," which means they may be amended. Isn't it possible that there could be a need to change some of the wording in these motions?

We will suppose that Member X made a motion to "postpone the question to our next meeting." Member O, however, feels that it should be postponed to a later meeting. What could Member O do? After recognition by the chairman, Member O would say, "Mr. Chairman, I move that we amend the motion to postpone by striking the word 'next' and inserting in its place the word 'February.' "

The chairman would ask for a second, and debate, after which he would bring the motion to amend the motion to postpone to a vote and then vote on the motion to postpone.

The same principle would apply to the motions to refer to committee and recess. A motion may be on the floor to "refer to a committee of five members," and someone else feels that the committee should have three members or seven members. Or a motion may be on the floor to "take a five-minute recess," and another member feels that if we have a recess it should be a one-minute or ten-minute recess. Thus the need for the "A" after each of these three types of motions.

If the motion to refer to committee is ADOPTED, the entire question, including any amendments, is given to the committee; or, in the cases of postponement, the entire question will come up under OLD BUSINESS at the time to which it was postponed.

One of the useful motions in parliamentary procedure is the motion to close debate. The more sophisticated phrase is: "I move the previous question." But since few people in today's society appear to have knowledge of any of the motions, I suggest using "I move that we close debate." These words are meaningful to almost anyone.

Perhaps you have heard members call out, "QUESTION, QUESTION." There is a popular belief that this is a demand that the chairman put the question to an immediate vote. The chairman will say, "The question has been called for, so we must bring the question to a vote. All in favor . . ."

I suggest to you that these people aren't even remotely aware of the democratic process, much less knowing anything about parliamentary procedure.

Assume that Member B is attending our PTA meeting tonight. He much preferred staying at home and watching the football game on television, but he was pressured into coming to the meeting instead. If he can get the meeting over in a hurry, though, he may still get home in time to catch the last half. So Member B calls out "Question" every time any motion is made. The chairman goes through his routine and the meeting is over in 30 minutes.

Was there full, free, and fair debate at this meeting? How many violations did Member B commit? First, he was supposed to be recognized by the presiding officer because there was nothing privileged about his "request." Second, since he was, in fact, making an implied motion to "close debate and get on with the voting," he needed a friend, who also wanted to get home and watch the ballgame, to second his motions. Third, not only does a motion require a vote, but the motion to close debate requires more than the normal number of votes—it requires a two-thirds vote to adopt.

Not only may just one person not stop the entire assembly from having full, free, and fair debate, but it takes twice as many voting "aye" as those voting "no" to stop it. Yet, in most circles, everyone accepts the procedure of one person calling "Question" and denying other members the right to speak.

If the motion is made to close debate, it refers to the immediately pending question, that is, the top-ranking motion on the floor (chart). If you wish to close debate on all motions on the floor, you must state: "I move the previous question on all pending motions." Or "I move we close debate on all pending motions."

Now let's assume the following motions are on the floor:

The immediately pending question is the motion to table the question.

If, when the vote is taken, the motion to table is adopted, what effect does this motion have? It is very simple! It means that the main motion, and all motions attached to it, goes into the secretary's book and stays there until or unless a member makes a motion to TAKE it FROM THE TABLE.

In the following chart, the motions that go into the table (secretary's book) are the main motion, the amendment, the amendment to the amendment, and the motion to postpone.

These motions can be put back on the floor later if a member makes a motion to take from the table. The member must be recognized by the chairmn, just as if he/she were making any other motion. The motion to take from the table, like the motion to table, must have a second (S), it is not debatable, not amendable, requires a majority (M) vote to adopt, and cannot be reconsidered.

The motion to take from the table may not be made until *after one item* of business has been transacted and may not be made after the adjournment of the following meeting (next month's meeting.) There are no requirements that a tabled motion must be taken from the table; but if it is not taken from the table before the adjournment of the following meeting, and you want the subject brought up again, you will have to bring it back in the form of a new main motion. The chairman never takes the initiative to bring a tabled motion from the table.

ADJOURN					
RECESS					
TABLE	S			M	
CLOSE DEBATE					
LIMIT DEBATE					
POSTPONE DEFINITELY	S	D	A	M	R
REFER TO COMMITTEE					
AMEND AMENDMENT	S	D		M	R
AMEND	S	D	A	M	R
POSTPONE INDEFINITELY					
MAIN MOTION	S	D	A	M	R

SEE REVERSE SIDE

DEFINITIONS:

"S" means the motion must be seconded.
"D" means it may be debated.
"A" means it may be amended.
"M" requires a majority vote to pass.
"2" means it takes a 2/3 vote to pass.
"R" after the motion has been voted on, it may be reconsidered.

DESIGN SERVICES OF MEMPHIS • 1702 Lawrence Pl. • Memphis, Tn. 38112 • Phone 901 / 278-6739

PRINTED IN U S A

Suppose that a member wants to bring the tabled motion back on the floor. One item of business has been transacted and the member is recognized by the presiding officer, after which he/she makes a motion to take from the table. The motion is duly seconded, voted on, and is adopted. Now, the chart is just as it was before the motion was tabled. The immediately pending question is the motion to postpone.

The motion to postpone failed. (The POSTPONE slide is moved to the right.)

The motion to amend the amendment was adopted. (Move this slide to the right.)

The motion to amend was adopted. (Move this slide to the right.)

The main motion (as amended) was adopted. (Move this slide to the right.)

This is the complete explanation of how tabling a motion operates: WHEN A MOTION IS TABLED, THE MAIN MOTION AND ALL OTHER MOTIONS ATTACHED TO IT GO TO THE TABLE TOGETHER.

WHEN A TABLED MOTION IS TAKEN FROM THE TABLE, ALL MOTIONS COME FROM THE TABLE AS IF THEY HAD NEVER BEEN TABLED IN THE FIRST PLACE.

It is important to be aware of the manner in which many of our elected officials use the motion to table. It is important because they will also be attending many of your meetings, you will be confronted with their version of the procedure, and you must not be intimidated by them.

As recently as December 1975, I heard a councilman tell the citizens on a radio talk show that he tried to table a motion to postpone, but it was voted down.

What is the logic of tabling a motion to postpone something?

ADJOURN

RECESS

TABLE

CLOSE DEBATE

LIMIT DEBATE

| POSTPONE DEFINITELY | S | D | A | M | R |

REFER TO COMMITTEE

| AMEND AMENDMENT | S | D | | M | R |

| AMEND | S | D | A | M | R |

POSTPONE INDEFINITELY

| MAIN MOTION | S | D | A | M | R |

SEE REVERSE SIDE

DEFINITIONS:

"S" means the motion must be seconded.
"D" means it may be debated.
"A" means it may be amended.
"M" requires a majority vote to pass.
"2" means it takes a 2/3 vote to pass.
"R" after the motion has been voted on, it may be reconsidered.

DESIGN SERVICES OF MEMPHIS • 1702 Lawrence Pl. • Memphis, Tn. 38112 • Phone 901 / 278-6739

PRINTED IN U S A

71

We'll take the hypothetical case that there is a motion on the floor to have an investigation of the corporation that has been awarded the franchise to bring Cable TV to our city. This is the main motion.

A member now makes a motion to postpone the question until the next meeting (postpone definitely).

The two motions on the floor, then, are the main motion and the motion to postpone definitely.

Lucille Place, CPP
Richard S. Kain, CPP

ADJOURN

RECESS

TABLE

CLOSE DEBATE

LIMIT DEBATE

POSTPONE DEFINITELY | S | D | A | M | R |

REFER TO COMMITTEE

AMEND AMENDMENT

AMEND

POSTPONE INDEFINITELY

MAIN MOTION | S | D | A | M | R |

SEE REVERSE SIDE

DEFINITIONS:

"S" means the motion must be seconded.
"D" means it may be debated.
"A" means it may be amended.
"M" requires a majority vote to pass.
"2" means it takes a 2/3 vote to pass.
"R" after the motion has been voted on, it may be reconsidered.

DESIGN SERVICES OF MEMPHIS • 1702 Lawrence Pl. • Memphis, Tn. 38112 • Phone 901 / 278-6739

PRINTED IN U S A

73

Next, a councilman makes a motion to table the motion to postpone. (The proper procedure is to table the main motion and, if it is adopted, the motion to postpone will automatically be tabled with it.)

The immediately pending question thus is, according to the councilman, the motion to "table the motion to postpone." Let's assume his motion is adopted and the motion to postpone is tabled (PLACED IN THE SECRETARY'S BOOK). According to the councilman's theory, then, we will move both the TABLE and POSTPONE slides to the right side of the chart.

ADJOURN

RECESS

TABLE | S | | M | |

CLOSE DEBATE

LIMIT DEBATE

POSTPONE DEFINITELY | S | D | A | M | R |

REFER TO COMMITTEE

AMEND AMENDMENT

AMEND

POSTPONE INDEFINITELY

MAIN MOTION | S | D | A | M | R |

SEE REVERSE SIDE

DEFINITIONS:

"S" means the motion must be seconded.
"D" means it may be debated.
"A" means it may be amended.
"M" requires a majority vote to pass.
"2" means it takes a 2/3 vote to pass.
"R" after the motion has been voted on, it may be reconsidered.

DESIGN SERVICES OF MEMPHIS • 1702 Lawrence Pl. • Memphis, Tn. 38112 • Phone 901 / 278-6739

PRINTED IN U.S.A.

75

The chart now looks like this:

The immediately pending question at this point is the main motion. The main motion is brought to a vote and is adopted by a majority vote. THE GROUP (the council) HAS VOTED TO INVESTIGATE THE CORPORATION THAT HAS THE CABLE TV FRANCHISE.

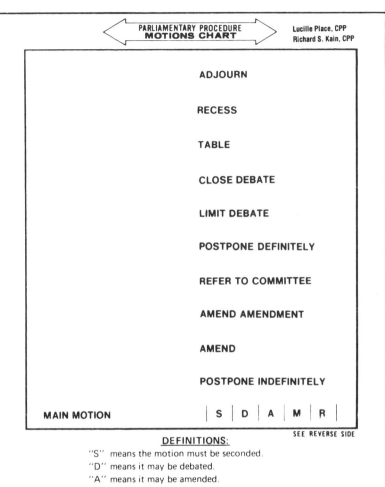

ADJOURN

RECESS

TABLE

CLOSE DEBATE

LIMIT DEBATE

POSTPONE DEFINITELY

REFER TO COMMITTEE

AMEND AMENDMENT

AMEND

POSTPONE INDEFINITELY

| MAIN MOTION | S | D | A | M | R |

SEE REVERSE SIDE

DEFINITIONS:

"S" means the motion must be seconded.

"D" means it may be debated.

"A" means it may be amended.

"M" requires a majority vote to pass.

"2" means it takes a 2/3 vote to pass.

"R" after the motion has been voted on, it may be reconsidered.

DESIGN SERVICES OF MEMPHIS • 1702 Lawrence Pl. • Memphis, Tn. 38112 • Phone 901 / 278-6739

PRINTED IN U S A

As one item of business has been transacted, according to the rules the tabled motion can be taken from the table by a majority vote. A councilman makes a motion to take from the table the motion that was tabled (the motion that is now in the secretary's book). This was the motion to postpone. The motion to take from the table is adopted. So we take the motion to postpone out of the secretary's book and put it back on the floor, and the CHART now looks like this:

The immediately pending question is "That we postpone the question until a future meeting." What question? If you're speaking of the question to investigate the corporation that has been awarded the Cable TV franchise, that question has already been disposed of; it was adopted. What is left to postpone?

What really happened here was that a councilman made a motion to investigate the Cable TV corporation (a main motion). Another councilman made the motion to postpone the main motion to a later meeting. The councilman who made the main motion didn't want his motion postponed; he wanted it acted on today. Instead of debating against the motion to postpone, trying to get the majority of the council to vote against that motion, he made a motion to table the motion to postpone. If the councilmen, by majority vote, adopted the motion to table, he thought, this would get the postponed motion out of the way and they could get on with his main motion. Much more logically, why not just vote against the motion to postpone instead of trying to table it?

Unfortunately, tabling in this fashion is too-common practice among elected officials. Beware it—do not ape it.

78

ADJOURN

RECESS

TABLE

CLOSE DEBATE

LIMIT DEBATE

POSTPONE DEFINITELY | S | D | A | M | R |

REFER TO COMMITTEE

AMEND AMENDMENT

AMEND

POSTPONE INDEFINITELY

MAIN MOTION

SEE REVERSE SIDE

DEFINITIONS:

"S" means the motion must be seconded.
"D" means it may be debated.
"A" means it may be amended.
"M" requires a majority vote to pass.
"2" means it takes a 2/3 vote to pass.
"R" after the motion has been voted on, it may be reconsidered.

DESIGN SERVICES OF MEMPHIS • 1702 Lawrence Pl. • Memphis, Tn. 38112 • Phone 901 / 278-6739

PRINTED IN U S A*

How to Dispose of Numerous Motions That Are Pending

The following motions are on the floor:

Perhaps you feel that it will take hours to dispose of so many motions. The time and difficulty involved depend on how much parliamentary procedure you know.

(I deliberately left out the motion to POSTPONE INDEFINITELY because I have only seen it used once during my 26 years of parliamentary activity. I feel, therefore, it is just one more thing to learn that you probably won't need. If you feel the need to use it, there are many books available that will explain it.)

PARLIAMENTARY PROCEDURE MOTIONS CHART						Lucille Place, CPP Richard S. Kain, CPP

ADJOURN	S			M	
RECESS	S		A	M	
TABLE	S			M	
CLOSE DEBATE	S			2	R

LIMIT DEBATE

POSTPONE DEFINITELY	S	D	A	M	R
REFER TO COMMITTEE	S	D	A	M	R
AMEND AMENDMENT	S	D		M	R
AMEND	S	D	A	M	R

POSTPONE INDEFINITELY

MAIN MOTION	S	D	A	M	R

SEE REVERSE SIDE

DEFINITIONS:

"S" means the motion must be seconded.
"D" means it may be debated.
"A" means it may be amended.
"M" requires a majority vote to pass.
"2" means it takes a 2/3 vote to pass.
"R" after the motion has been voted on, it may be reconsidered.

DESIGN SERVICES OF MEMPHIS • 1702 Lawrence Pl. • Memphis, Tn. 38112 • Phone 901 / 278-6739

PRINTED IN U.S.A

81

The immediately pending question is the motion to adjourn. There is no (D), so it is not debatable and must be voted on immediately.

Chairman: "The immediately pending question is the motion to adjourn. The motion is not debatable and requires a majority vote.... All in favor say 'aye.' ... Those opposed say 'no.' ... The motion is lost." The AD-JOURN slide is pushed to the right and the chart now looks like this:

Lucille Place, CPP
Richard S. Kain, CPP

	S	D	A	M / 2	R
ADJOURN					
RECESS	S		A	M	
TABLE	S			M	
CLOSE DEBATE	S			2	R
LIMIT DEBATE					
POSTPONE DEFINITELY	S	D	A	M	R
REFER TO COMMITTEE	S	D	A	M	R
AMEND AMENDMENT	S	D		M	R
AMEND	S	D	A	M	R
POSTPONE INDEFINITELY					
MAIN MOTION	S	D	A	M	R

SEE REVERSE SIDE

DEFINITIONS:

"S" means the motion must be seconded.
"D" means it may be debated.
"A" means it may be amended.
"M" requires a majority vote to pass.
"2" means it takes a 2/3 vote to pass.
"R" after the motion has been voted on, it may be reconsidered.

DESIGN SERVICES OF MEMPHIS • 1702 Lawrence Pl. • Memphis, Tn 38112 • Phone 901 / 278-6739

PRINTED IN U.S.A.

The immediately pending question is the motion to recess for ten minutes.

Chairman: "The immediately pending question is the motion to recess for ten minutes. This motion is not debatable and requires a majority vote to adopt. . . . All in favor say 'aye.' . . . Those opposed say 'no.' . . . The motion is adopted and we will reconvene at 2:10." (There is an (A) on the chart that means that some member could have made a motion to amend the motion by striking "ten minutes" and inserting "thirty minutes," etc.) The RECESS slide is pushed to the right and the chart looks like this:

The immediately pending question is the motion to table. (Recess is over and the meeting has reconvened.)

Chairman: "The immediately pending question is the motion to table. This motion is not debatable and requires a majority vote to adopt. All in favor say 'aye.' . . . Those opposed say 'no.' . . . The motion lost."

ADJOURN

RECESS

TABLE	S			M	
CLOSE DEBATE	S			2	R

LIMIT DEBATE

POSTPONE DEFINITELY	S	D	A	M	R
REFER TO COMMITTEE	S	D	A	M	R
AMEND AMENDMENT	S	D		M	R
AMEND	S	D	A	M	R

POSTPONE INDEFINITELY

MAIN MOTION	S	D	A	M	R

SEE REVERSE SIDE

DEFINITIONS:

"S" means the motion must be seconded.

"D" means it may be debated.

"A" means it may be amended.

"M" requires a majority vote to pass.

"2" means it takes a 2/3 vote to pass.

"R" after the motion has been voted on, it may be reconsidered.

DESIGN SERVICES OF MEMPHIS • 1702 Lawrence Pl. • Memphis, Tn. 38112 • Phone 901 / 278-6739

PRINTED IN U.S.A.

The TABLE slide is pushed to the right and the chart now looks like this:

The immediately pending question is the motion to close debate.

Chairman: "The immediately pending question is the motion to close debate. This motion is not debatable and requires a two-thirds vote to adopt [twice as many voting 'aye' as those voting 'no']. All in favor of the motion to close debate raise your hand. . . . Those opposed raise your hand. . . . The motion is adopted."

When a motion is made to close debate (or previous question), it applies only to the immediately pending question (motion); that is, in this case it would be the motion to postpone because it is the next motion down the ladder. If the member who made the motion wanted to close debate on all motions, the member would have said, "I move to close debate on all pending motions."

ADJOURN

RECESS

TABLE

| CLOSE DEBATE | S | | | 2 | R |

LIMIT DEBATE

| POSTPONE DEFINITELY | S | D | A | M | R |

| REFER TO COMMITTEE | S | D | A | M | R |

| AMEND AMENDMENT | S | D | | M | R |

| AMEND | S | D | A | M | R |

POSTPONE INDEFINITELY

| MAIN MOTION | S | D | A | M | R |

SEE REVERSE SIDE

DEFINITIONS:

"S" means the motion must be seconded.
"D" means it may be debated.
"A" means it may be amended.
"M" requires a majority vote to pass.
"2" means it takes a 2/3 vote to pass.
"R" after the motion has been voted on, it may be reconsidered.

DESIGN SERVICES OF MEMPHIS • 1702 Lawrence Pl. • Memphis, Tn. 38112 • Phone 901 / 278-6739

PRINTED IN U.S.A

87

The CLOSE DEBATE slide is pushed to the right and the chart appears so:

The immediately pending question is the motion to postpone.

Chairman: "The immediately pending question is the motion to postpone the question until our next meeting. The motion is normally debatable, but the assembly just adopted a motion to close debate on this motion, so we will vote immediately. All in favor say 'aye.' ... Those opposed say 'no.' ... The motion fails."

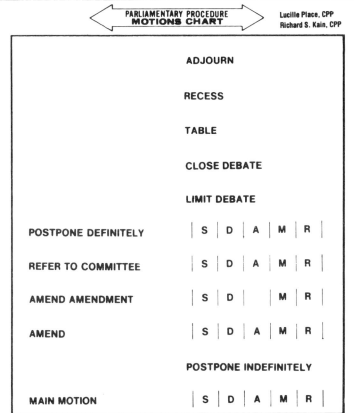

ADJOURN

RECESS

TABLE

CLOSE DEBATE

LIMIT DEBATE

POSTPONE DEFINITELY	S	D	A	M	R
REFER TO COMMITTEE	S	D	A	M	R
AMEND AMENDMENT	S	D		M	R
AMEND	S	D	A	M	R
POSTPONE INDEFINITELY					
MAIN MOTION	S	D	A	M	R

SEE REVERSE SIDE

DEFINITIONS:

"S" means the motion must be seconded.
"D" means it may be debated.
"A" means it may be amended.
"M" requires a majority vote to pass.
"2" means it takes a 2/3 vote to pass.
"R" after the motion has been voted on, it may be reconsidered.

DESIGN SERVICES OF MEMPHIS • 1702 Lawrence Pl. • Memphis, Tn. 38112 • Phone 901 / 278-6739

PRINTED IN U.S.A.

The POSTPONE slide is pushed to the right and the chart looks like this:

The immediately pending question is the motion to refer to committee.

Chairman: "The immediately pending question is the motion to refer the question to a committee. The motion is debatable, amendable, and requires only a majority vote to adopt. Is there any further debate? (Since the motion to close debate was not qualified, it referred only to the previous question, the motion to postpone, as mentioned before.) . . . Hearing none, we will now vote. . . . All in favor say 'aye.' . . . Those opposed say 'no.' . . . The motion failed."

ADJOURN

RECESS

TABLE

CLOSE DEBATE

LIMIT DEBATE

POSTPONE DEFINITELY

REFER TO COMMITTEE	S	D	A	M	R
AMEND AMENDMENT	S	D		M	R
AMEND	S	D	A	M	R
POSTPONE INDEFINITELY					
MAIN MOTION	S	D	A	M	R

SEE REVERSE SIDE

DEFINITIONS:

"S" means the motion must be seconded.
"D" means it may be debated.
"A" means it may be amended.
"M" requires a majority vote to pass.
"2" means it takes a 2/3 vote to pass.
"R" after the motion has been voted on, it may be reconsidered.

DESIGN SERVICES OF MEMPHIS • 1702 Lawrence Pl. • Memphis, Tn. 38112 • Phone 901 / 278-6739

PRINTED IN U S A

The REFER TO COMMITTEE slide is pushed to the right and the chart looks like this:

The immediately pending question is the amendment to the amendment.

Chairman: "The immediately pending question now is the motion to amend the amendment, which is to add the words 'at Overton Park.' The main motion is 'that the club have a picnic.' The amendment is to add the words 'at 2:30 on Sunday afternoon,' and the amendment to the amendment is to add the words 'at Overton Park.' The only debate at this time is on the feasibility of the Overton Park site. Is there any debate? . . . Hearing none, we will vote. All in favor say 'aye.' . . . All opposed say 'no.' . . . The motion is adopted."

ADJOURN

RECESS

TABLE

CLOSE DEBATE

LIMIT DEBATE

POSTPONE DEFINITELY

REFER TO COMMITTEE

	S	D		M	R
AMEND AMENDMENT	S	D		M	R
AMEND	S	D	A	M	R

POSTPONE INDEFINITELY

	S	D	A	M	R
MAIN MOTION	S	D	A	M	R

SEE REVERSE SIDE

DEFINITIONS:

"S" means the motion must be seconded.
"D" means it may be debated.
"A" means it may be amended.
"M" requires a majority vote to pass.
"2" means it takes a 2/3 vote to pass.
"R" after the motion has been voted on, it may be reconsidered.

DESIGN SERVICES OF MEMPHIS • 1702 Lawrence Pl. • Memphis, Tn. 38112 • Phone 901 / 278-6739

PRINTED IN U.S.A.

93

The AMEND AMENDMENT slide is pushed to the right and the chart looks thus:

The immediately pending question is the motion to amend.

Chairman: "The immediately pending question now is the motion to amend by adding the words 'at 2:30 on Sunday afternoon . . . at Overton Park.' Is there further discussion on the amendment as it has been amended? The only discussion at this time is whether you like the time and the site. Is there further discussion (debate)? . . . Hearing none, we will vote. All in favor say 'aye.' . . . Those opposed say 'no.' . . . The motion is adopted."

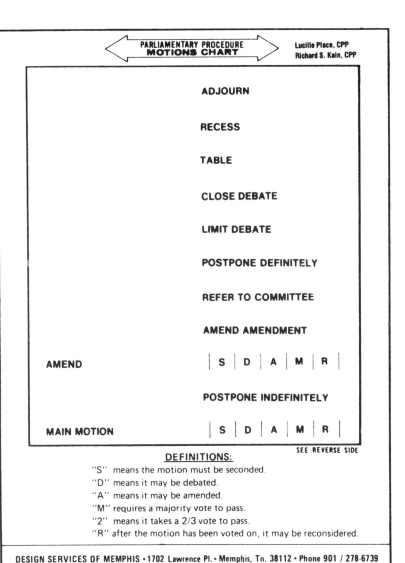

ADJOURN

RECESS

TABLE

CLOSE DEBATE

LIMIT DEBATE

POSTPONE DEFINITELY

REFER TO COMMITTEE

AMEND AMENDMENT

AMEND | S | D | A | M | R |

POSTPONE INDEFINITELY

MAIN MOTION | S | D | A | M | R |

SEE REVERSE SIDE

DEFINITIONS:
"S" means the motion must be seconded.
"D" means it may be debated.
"A" means it may be amended.
"M" requires a majority vote to pass.
"2" means it takes a 2/3 vote to pass.
"R" after the motion has been voted on, it may be reconsidered.

DESIGN SERVICES OF MEMPHIS • 1702 Lawrence Pl. • Memphis, Tn. 38112 • Phone 901 / 278-6739

PRINTED IN U S A

95

The AMEND slide is moved to the right and the chart looks pretty bare:

The immediately pending question is the main motion (which has been amended twice).

Chairman: "The immediately pending question is the main motion that has been amended twice. The motion now reads: 'That the club have a picnic . . . at 2:30 on Sunday afternoon . . . at Overton Park.' Is there further debate on the main motion? . . . Hearing none, we will vote. All in favor say 'aye.' . . . Those opposed say 'no.' . . .

ADJOURN

RECESS

TABLE

CLOSE DEBATE

LIMIT DEBATE

POSTPONE DEFINITELY

REFER TO COMMITTEE

AMEND AMENDMENT

AMEND

POSTPONE INDEFINITELY

MAIN MOTION | S | D | A | M | R |

SEE REVERSE SIDE

• DEFINITIONS:

"S" means the motion must be seconded.

"D" means it may be debated.

"A" means it may be amended.

"M" requires a majority vote to pass.

"2" means it takes a 2/3 vote to pass.

"R" after the motion has been voted on, it may be reconsidered.

DESIGN SERVICES OF MEMPHIS • 1702 Lawrence Pl. • Memphis, Tn. 38112 • Phone 901 / 278-6739

PRINTED IN U.S.A.

97

The motion is adopted. The chair appoints Members A, B, E, J, and M to a committee to implement the motion."
  The CHART now looks like this:

  Chairman: "Is there further business to come before this assembly?"

PARLIAMENTARY PROCEDURE
MOTIONS CHART

Lucille Place, CPP
Richard S. Kain, CPP

ADJOURN

RECESS

TABLE

CLOSE DEBATE

LIMIT DEBATE

POSTPONE DEFINITELY

REFER TO COMMITTEE

AMEND AMENDMENT

AMEND

POSTPONE INDEFINITELY

MAIN MOTION

SEE REVERSE SIDE

DEFINITIONS:

"S" means the motion must be seconded.
"D" means it may be debated.
"A" means it may be amended.
"M" requires a majority vote to pass.
"2" means it takes a 2/3 vote to pass.
"R" after the motion has been voted on, it may be reconsidered.

DESIGN SERVICES OF MEMPHIS • 1702 Lawrence Pl. • Memphis, Tn. 38112 • Phone 901 / 278-6739

Part III

ANSWERS TO THE QUESTIONS ON PARLIAMENTARY SITUATIONS

MAIN MOTION

1. *YOU WANT TO BRING A NEW IDEA BEFORE THE GROUP*—What would you do?

   > After recognition by the chair, make a main motion.
   >
   > Member: "Mister Chairman, I move that we have a picnic."
   >
   > Chairman: "Is there a second?" [If not, the motion dies.] After the motion has been seconded, the chairman must repeat the motion.
   >
   > Chairman: "A motion has been made and seconded that we have a picnic. Is there any discussion?" When the discussion is over, the chairman puts the question (motion) to a vote.
   >
   > Chairman: "All in favor of the motion [repeat the motion if there is any concern that the members do not know what they are voting on] say 'aye,' [pause for vote]. All opposed say 'no.'"
   >
   > The presiding officer (chairman) must always announce the results of the vote.
   >
   > Chairman: "The motion is adopted," or "The motion failed."

OBJECTION TO CONSIDERING

2. *YOU DO NOT WANT AN IDEA, JUST INTRODUCED BY ANOTHER MEMBER, DISCUSSED AT All*—What would you do?

   > Rise immediately, without recognition by the presiding officer and *before* one word of discussion has begun, and object. (You may wish to wait to see if the motion gets a second; if not, it will die anyway.)
   >
   > Member: "Mister Chairman, I OBJECT TO THE CONSIDERATION of this question (motion)." No second is required, and the chairman must bring this question to a vote immediately. You must remember, however, that objections can be made on main motions only. After one word of debate, or the attach-

ment of subsidiary motions, the assembly is, in fact, considering it and it is too late to object.

Chairman: "There has been an objection to this motion; the objection requires no second, it is not debatable, and it requires a two-thirds vote *against* considering the motion, which is 'that the club support Jack the Ripper for governor.' Those who wish to consider the motion, raise your hands [pause for vote]. Those who do not wish to consider the motion, raise your hands [pause for vote]."

If there were twice as many hands raised that opposed considering the motion as those that wished to consider it, the motion cannot be considered. When there is need for a two-thirds vote for passage, the vote must be taken by a voice vote. After the vote, the chairman states: "There were not twice as many votes against considering the motion, so the motion will be considered."

AMENDING, AND AN AMENDMENT TO THE AMENDMENT

3. *YOU WANT TO CHANGE SOME OF THE WORDING IN AN IDEA THAT IS BEING DISCUSSED*—What would you do?

The main motion, "to have a picnic and dance," is on the floor and is now being discussed. After recognition by the presiding officer, you make a motion to amend. A motion can be amended in only three ways: (1) add a word (or words); (2) strike a word (or words); or (3) strike a word (or words) and in its (their) place insert a word (or words).

(1) ADDING example:

Member: "Madam Chairman, I move that the main motion be amended by adding the words 'at Overton Park.'"

(2) STRIKING example:

Member: "Madam Chairman, I move that the main motion be amended by striking the word 'dance.'"

(3) STRIKING and INSERTING example:

Member: "Madam Chairman, I move that the main motion be amended by striking the word 'picnic' and inserting in its place the word 'dinner.'"

The Chairman asks: "is there a second to the motion to amend? . . . A motion has been made and seconded that the main motion be amended by adding the words 'at Overton Park.' Is there any discussion?"

Chairman: " . . . A motion has been made and seconded that the main motion be amended by striking the word 'picnic' and inserting in its place the word 'dinner.' Is there any debate?"

Perhaps, during the discussion, a member wants to amend the amendment. The amendment can be amended in the same manner as the main motion was amended.

EXAMPLE:

Member: "Mister Chairman, I move that the amendment be amended by adding the words 'to be held March 15th.'"

Chairman: "A motion has been made and seconded that the amendment be amended by adding the words 'to be held March 15th.' is there any debate?"

REFER TO A COMMITTEE

4. *YOU WANT MORE STUDY AND INVESTIGATION GIVEN THE IDEA THAT IS BEING DISCUSSED*—What would you do?

After recognition by the presiding officer, make a motion to refer the question to a committee.

Member: "Mister Chairman, I move that this question

be referred to a committee."

Chairman: "Is there a second? ... A motion has been made and seconded that this question be referred to a committee. Is there any debate? The debate at this time must be confined to the feasibility, or lack of it, of referring to a committee, and cannot go into the main motion."

Look at the chart. Isn't there an (A) opposite the REFER TO COMMITTEE slide? This means the motion to refer can be amended.

Member: (after recognition) "Mr. Chairman, I move that the motion to refer to a committee be amended by adding the words 'and that the committee shall consist of members A, B, T, and Y.'" The Chairman must ask for a second, repeat the motion to amend the motion to refer to a committee and ask for debate. The motion to amend is voted on first, and then the motion to refer to a committee (with amendment attached, if the amendment was adopted) is voted on. If the motion to refer to committee fails, then the main motion is the immediately pending question and must be disposed of (voted on).

POSTPONE DEFINITELY (To a Certain Time)

5. *YOU WANT MORE TIME TO STUDY THE SUBJECT; YOU MAY WANT TO SUGGEST ANOTHER DAY, OR EVEN A PARTICULAR HOUR, TO BRING IT BACK FOR DISCUSSION*—What would you do?

After recognition by the Chairman, make a motion to POSTPONE DEFINITELY (to a certain time).

Member: "Mister Chairman, I move that we postpone this question until our next meeting on January 6."

Chairman: "Is there a second? ... A motion has been made and seconded that we postpone this question until our January 6th meeting. Is there any debate?"

Look at the chart. Isn't there an (A) opposite the POSTPONE DEFINITELY slide? This means that the motion to postpone may be amended. Isn't it logical to assume that a member may wish to strike "January 6" and insert "February 7" or some other time? If there is a motion to amend the motion to postpone, it is handled in the same manner as the motion to amend the motion to refer to committee (see situation number 4).

Suppose, however, you are attending a three-day convention and the assembly is discussing the construction of a multi-million-dollar national headquarters. Questions have arisen concerning matters that only the architect can answer. You have just been advised that the architect will be available tomorrow at 2:30 P.M., but can stay no longer than 15 minutes. What would you do?

Member: (after recognition by the presiding officer) "Mr. Chairman, I move that the question be postponed to tomorrow at 2:30 P.M. and that it be made a SPECIAL ORDER." This motion needs a second (S) and is debatable (D), but requires a two-thirds (2) vote instead of a majority vote. Why? Because the special order requires that, regardless of what is on the floor at 2:30, it must step aside so that the architect may answer the questions. (After which, this motion can go back to the floor.) If the motion to postpone had not included the words "special order," it would have taken only a majority vote, and whatever would be on the floor at 2:30 must be disposed of before the motion that was postponed could be considered.

LIMITING DEBATE—PREVIOUS QUESTION
(Close Debate)

6. *YOU ARE TIRED OF LISTENING TO SO MUCH DISCUSSION; OR YOU MAY WANT TO SUGGEST A LIMIT TO THE DISCUSSION*—What would you do?

After recognition by the presiding officer, make a motion to close debate or to limit debate.

Member: "Mr. Chairman, I move the previous question." Or, "I move that we close debate." Or, "I move that we limit the debate on this entire question to ten more minutes." Or, "I move that the debate be limited to four more speakers, two for and two against the motion, alternating for and against the motion, and that each speaker be limited to two minutes."

Chairman: "Is there a second? . . . A motion has been made and seconded that we close debate. This motion is not debatable and requires a two-thirds vote (2) to adopt. All in favor of closing debate raise your hand [pause for vote]. Those opposed to closing debate raise your hand [pause for vote]. Since there were twice as many voting for the motion to close debate, the motion is adopted and debate has been closed. We are now ready to vote on the immediately pending question, which is . . ."

Let's assume there were several motions on the floor, that is, a main motion, an amendment to the main motion, and a motion to refer to committee. Now, if the maker of the motion to close debate merely says, "I move the previous question" or "I move that we close debate," this means that he/she only wants to close debate on the immediately pending motion, which is the motion to refer to committee, and not on the other two motions. If you are tired of listening to the debate of the whole thing, you must say, "I move that we close debate on *all* pending motions." If this motion is adopted, the votes on all motions will be taken immediately. (In other words, you will vote on each motion, one at a time, going down the chart.)

LAY ON THE TABLE (Table)
TAKE FROM THE TABLE

7. *YOU WANT TO FORGET ABOUT THE IDEA FOR A WHILE, BUT YOU MAY WANT IT BROUGHT BACK FOR DISCUSSION AT A LATER TIME*—What would you do?

After recognition by the chairman, you make a motion to table (lay on the table) the question of XYZ.

Member: "Madam Chairman, I move that we lay the question of XYZ on the table" or "Madam Chairman, I move that we table the question of XYZ." In plain everyday language you are saying, "Madam Chairman, I move that we put this motion in the secretary's book and forget about it." (The motion is disregarded until or unless a member wants to bring it back to the floor. The motion to take from the table may *not* be made until *after* one item of business has been transacted, and may not be made *after* the adjournment of the following meeting (next month's meeting.)

The motion to take from the table has the same requirements as the motion to lay on the table. They both require recognition by the chair; they must be seconded (S); cannot be debated; cannot be amended; require a majority (M) vote to adopt, and cannot be reconsidered.

There are no requirements that a tabled motion must be taken from the table; but it is not taken from the table before the adjournment of the following meeting, and you want the subject back on the floor, you will have to bring it back in the form of a new main motion. The chairman never takes the initiative to bring a tabled motion from the table.

Chairman: "Is there a second? . . . A motion has been made and seconded that the question of XYZ be tabled. The motion to table is not debatable, it cannot be amended, and it requires a majority vote to adopt.

109

The vote cannot be reconsidered after it has been taken. All in favor say 'aye' [pause for vote]. Those opposed say 'no' . . . The motion is adopted and the question has been tabled."

IMPORTANT: When the motion to table is adopted, the main motion and all motions attached to it go to the table (the secretary's book). In other words, a subsidiary motion, such as a motion to postpone definitely (to a certain time), cannot be tabled. If the motion to postpone definitely is attached to a main motion, then it goes to the table with the main motion, but it cannot be tabled alone.

For example, there is a motion on the floor to "have a picnic" and someone makes a motion to postpone the motion to have a picnic to the next meeting, and another person makes a motion to table. This means the last member wants to table the main motion, but the motion to postpone will go to the table with it. YOU TABLE ALL OR NOTHING.

The motion to table was designed to lay a question aside temporarily, but it is, in fact, used to kill main motions. When it is used to kill a motion, it is my opinion that it should require a two-thirds vote to adopt. If you agree, then I suggest your organization adopt a standing rule, which has priority over your parliamentary authority, that would require a two-thirds vote. Otherwise, since the accepted parliamentary authorities require only a majority vote, you have no other choices.

If the motion to take from the table is adopted, the motion or motions come back to the floor just as if they had never been tabled in the first place.

RECESS

8.   *YOU WANT A SHORT BREAK, OR MAYBE EVEN A LONG BREAK*—What would you do?

   After recognition by the presiding officer, you make a motion to recess.

   Member: "Madam Chairman, I move that we have a five-minute recess."

   Chairman: "Is there a second? . . . A motion has been made and seconded that we have a five minute recess. This motion is not debatable and requires a majority vote to adopt. All in favor say 'aye' [pause for vote]. Those opposed say 'no.' . . . The motion is adopted and we will reconvene at 2:50."

   Look at the chart. Isn't there an (A) across from the RECESS slide? This means that the motion to recess may be amended. Isn't it logical to assume that a member may wish to strike "five" and insert "ten" or some other number of minutes? If there is a motion to amend the motion to recess, it is handled just as it is handled in the motion to amend the motions to refer to committee and postpone definitely (situations number 4 and 5).

ADJOURNMENT

9.   *YOU WANT THE MEETING TO END*—What would you do?

   After recognition by the presiding officer, you make a motion to adjourn.

   Member: "Madam Chairman, I move that we adjourn" or "I move that the meeting be adjourned."

   Chairman: "Is there a second? . . . A motion has been made and seconded that we adjourn. This motion is not debatable and requires a majority (M) vote to adopt. All in favor say 'aye' [pause for vote]. All opposed say 'no.' . . . The motion is adopted and you are adjourned."

111

It makes no difference, with a motion to adjourn, if it is the top motion on the chart (that is, made when a main motion is on the floor) or if it is made when there is no main motion. In either case the procedure is identical: it must be seconded (S), it is not debatable, it cannot be amended, and it requires a majority vote (M) to carry.

The only exceptions are: (a) When the assembly has voted for a time to adjourn, such as 4:00 P.M., and you want to change the time to 3:00 P.M.; (2) when no time has been set to adjourn, but you have stated a *time* in your motion to adjourn (this motion cannot be made when there is a main motion on the floor); and (3) when the adjournment will dissolve the assembly, as in a mass meeting or in the last meeting of a convention.

When these three situations arise, the adjourn motion takes on all the qualifications of any other main motion except that it cannot be reconsidered. This is quite simply because if the motion is adopted you go home; if it fails someone will eventually make a new motion to adjourn.

ADJOURNED MEETING

10. *YOU REALIZE THE CLUB'S BUSINESS CANNOT BE COMPLETED WITHIN THE ABSOLUTE TIME LIMIT FOR THIS MEETING, YET THERE ARE THINGS THAT MUST BE DONE BEFORE NEXT MONTH'S MEETING—* What would you do?

After recognition by the presiding officer, make a motion to have an adjourned meeting.

Member: "Mr. Chairman, I move that we adjourn this meeting to 7:00 P.M. tomorrow."

Chairman: "Is there a second? ... A motion has been made and seconded that we adjourn this meeting to 7:00 P.M. tomorrow. This motion is debatable (D) and amendable (A), and requires a majority (M) vote to adopt. All in favor say 'aye' [pause for vote]. Those opposed say 'no' [pause for vote]. The motion is adopted and you are adjourned until tomorrow at 7:00 P.M."

The motion is amendable because another member may prefer another time or another day and time. See situations 4, 5, and 8 that explain how to amend a subsidiary motion, such as the motion to refer to committee, to postpone definitely, and to recess.

The rationale behind the motion to have an adjourned meeting is that a regular or special meeting may not be able to complete the business and needs an extension of the meeting. An adjourned meeting takes up its work at the point where it was interrupted in the order of business, just as if it had never adjourned, except that the minutes of the preceding meeting are first read. A QUORUM (the number of people required to have a legal meeting) is also necessary at an adjourned meeting. As a matter of fact, all requirements for a regular or special meeting apply equally to an adjourned meeting.

DIVISION OF ASSEMBLY

11. *A VOTE WAS JUST TAKEN, BUT YOU WEREN'T SURE ABOUT THE RESULTS OF THE VOTE. THE PRESIDING OFFICER ANNOUNCED THAT THE MOTION WAS ADOPTED, BUT YOU THOUGHT YOU HEARD MORE "NO" VOTES THAN "YES" VOTES*—What would you do?
Without recognition by the presiding officer, just call out "DIVISION."

Member: "Division" or "I call for a division."
This is a demand that the presiding officer (chair) take a rising vote immediately.
Chairman: "Division has been called for And we will take a standing vote on the question. All in favor

please stand. . . . Please be seated. All opposed please stand. The motion is adopted."

Either the chairman, on his own initiative, or the assembly, by a majority vote, can order such a vote to be counted. If there is any doubt as to whether the motion passed, however, the chairman should appoint tellers (if the group is large in number) and count the votes.

PERMISSION TO WITHDRAW A MOTION

12.   *YOU JUST OFFERED AN IDEA TO THE GROUP AND IT IS BEING DISCUSSED,* YET *YOU WISH YOU HADN'T—* What would you do?

If you brought the subject before the assembly, then you made the motion. After your motion was seconded, and stated by the chair, the motion no longer belongs to you but to the assembly. You must, therefore, ask permission to withdraw the motion.

Member: (after recognition by the chair) "Mister Chairman, I ask permission to withdraw my motion."

Chairman: "If there is no objection, we will allow the maker of this motion to withdraw the motion. [Pause.] Hearing none, the motion is withdrawn."

In this simple case, the secretary, when transcribing his/her minutes, will not make mention either of the original motion or of the fact it was withdrawn.

If there is an objection to withdrawing the motion, the presiding officer may ask the members to vote on whether they will allow the member to withdraw his motion; or another member can, after recognition by the chair, make a motion as follows:

Member: "I move that the member be given permission to withdraw the motion." An immediate vote is taken and requires a majority vote to adopt. No second is needed because it is obvious that there are two members in favor of the motion to withdraw.

114

13a. *AT THE BEGINNING OF THE MEETING THE GROUP DECIDED WHICH SUBJECTS THEY WANTED TO BRING UP FIRST, BUT THE CHAIRMAN ISN'T FOLLOWING THIS PICTURE*—What would you do?

Before explaining the answer I will give you a sample AGENDA that the assembly presumably adopted:

Call to order

Reading and Approval of Minutes

Reports of Officers, Boards, and Standing Committees (Treasurer's report is one of the officers' reports) Reports of Special Committees

Special Orders

Unfinished Business

1. Valentine dance postponed from last meeting.

New Business

1. Discussion regarding an increase in dues

2. Discussion regarding the purchase of new typewriter

3. Proposal for purchase of new headquarters

Announcements

Adjournment

Let's assume the secretary has just completed the reading of the minutes and the chair announces, "The assembly will now take up the question of the Valentine dance." Without waiting for recognition CALL FOR THE ORDERS OF THE DAY.

Member: "Call for the orders of the day."

Chairman: "The orders of the day have been called for and we shall return to the adopted agenda."

Call for the orders of the day is a demand that the chairman adhere to the adopted agenda. If, however, the above agenda was not voted on by the assembly, then it is *not* the orders of the day. The agenda should be adopted at the beginning of each meeting.

SUSPENDING THE RULES

13b. *SUPPOSE, HOWEVER, IT HAS BECOME APPARENT TO YOU THAT ITEM #3, UNDER NEW BUSINESS, SHOULD BE CONSIDERED BEFORE ITEM #1 (THE AGENDA HAS BEEN ADOPTED*—What would you do?

>After recognition by the chairman, make a motion to SUSPEND THE RULES.

>Member: "Madam Chairman, I move that the rules be suspended (or that we suspend the rules) and insert Item #3 under new business ahead of Item #1."

>Chairman: "Is there a second? ... A motion has been made and seconded that we suspend the rules and insert Item #3 under 'new business' ahead of Item #1. The motion is not debatable and requires a two-thirds vote to adopt. All in favor raise your hands . . . [pause]. Those opposed raise your hands . . .[pause]. The motion is adopted. Item #3 now becomes Item #1 and items #1 and #2 become #2 and #3."

POINT OF PERSONAL PRIVILEGE

14. *THE MEETING HAS BECOME SO NOISY YOU CAN'T HEAR (OR YOU ARE TOO HOT OR TOO COLD); UNLESS SOMETHING IS DONE YOU MIGHT AS WELL GO HOME BECAUSE YOU ARE NOT GETTING ANYTHING OUT OF THE MEETING*—What would you do?

>Without waiting to be recognized by the chair, call out, "POINT OF PERSONAL PRIVILEGE."

>Member: "Point of personal privilege, Mister Chairman."

>Chairman: "State your point."

>Member: "There is so much talking around me that I can't hear the speaker(s)."

>Chairman: "Will anyone who wishes to speak, please address his remarks to the chair and not to those sitting around him. It is disturbing to the meeting," or "Will the sergeant-at-arms see that the heat is turned up (or the air conditioner turned down)."

116

All comments must be directed to the chair.
POINT OF GENERAL PRIVILEGE may be used when something is is the interest of the entire membership.

POINT OF INFORMATION
POINT OF ORDER

14b. *YOU ARE CONFUSED ABOUT THE PROCEDURES THAT ARE BEING USED AND YOU WANT SOME CLARIFICATION*—What would you do?

Without waiting for recognition from the chair, call out, "POINT OF INFORMATION," or "POINT OF PARLIAMENTARY INQUIRY."

The chairman asks you to state your point. Again you explain your problem. The inquiry must be relevant and of such importance to interrupt a speaker or the chairman may rule your point out of order. If none of the above points are satisfactory, you may wanrt to say "POINT OF ORDER." This is used when something, in your opinion, is completely out of hand and you wish emphatically to call it to the attention of the chairman.

APPEAL FROM THE DECISION OF THE CHAIR

14c. *THE CHAIRMAN JUST MADE A RULING AND YOU DON'T AGREE WITH THE RULING*—What would you do?

Without being recognized by the chair, call out, "Mister Chairman, I APPEAL FROM THE DECISION OF THE CHAIR." The appeal requires a second.

Chairman: "Is there a second to the appeal? . . . Will the member please state his appeal? [What did the Chair do that you feel was wrong?]"

Member: (State the error that you feel was made by the chairman.)

Chairman: (if the chair agrees with you) "The chair stands corrected. Thank you for bringing this to the chair's attention."

If the chair does not agree with you and still feels that the ruling was correct, the chairman will give his/her reasons for making the ruling and ask you if you still press your appeal.

Member: "Yes, I still press my appeal."

Since neither you nor the chair yields to the other, the members decide by majority vote which one they feel is correct. If the appeal involved a debatable subject, the appeal is debatable; if not, then the appeal is not debatable. After the assembly has debated it (if it is debatable), the appeal is brought to a vote.

Chairman: "Those who agree with the decision of the chair say 'aye'...[pause]. Those who do not agree with the decision of the chair, say 'no.'... The decision of the chair is upheld (sustained)." A tie vote will sustain the chair's decision. It will take a majority vote to overrule the chair's decision.

CREATING BLANKS AND FILLING BLANKS

15. *SOMEONE BRINGS UP THE IDEA OF BUYING THE PAST PRESIDENT A GIFT AND SUGGESTS THE CLUB PAY $500 FOR IT. YOU DON'T WANT TO SPEND MORE THAN $1.50; SOME OF THE OTHER MEMBERS ARE DISCUSSING OTHER AMOUNTS. THE SHOUTING BE-GAN 30 MINUTES AGO AND THEY ARE STILL UN-DECIDED ABOUT THE AMOUNT*—What would you do?

There is a motion on the floor that reads: "That the club purchase a $500 gift for the past president." Several other amounts have been suggested, but to amend the motion by "striking" and "inserting" the many different amounts suggested could keep you there all day.

After recognition by the chairman, make a motion to CREATE A BLANK.

Member: "Mister Chairman, I move that a blank be created to determine the amount to be spent on the gift."

Chairman: "Is there a second? . . . a motion has been made and seconded to create a blank. The motion is not debatable and it requires a majority (M) vote to adopt. All in favor say 'aye.' . . . Those opposed say 'no.' . . . The motion is adopted."

The motion now reads "That the club purchase a _____ gift for the past president."

The blank is filled in as if it were by an election. The chairman asks for suggestions (nominations) from the members of the assembly. After suggestions are made they may be debated; that is, reasons given for submitting the amount suggested. After all suggestions are made and discussed, they are voted on just as you would when electing someone to an office. If none of the figures receives a majority vote, then there must be a run-off between the two getting the highest numbers of votes.

Assume the suggestions were $500, $300, $150, $100, and $15; the votes were 85, 100, 75, 150, and 20. The 150 votes is a plurality, but not a majority of all votes cast, so the $100 (150 votes) and the $300 (100 votes) must be voted on again, and obviously one of them will get a majority. We'll assume the votes were 120 for $300 and 310 for $100, so the blank will therefore be filled by $100.

The motion now reads "That the club purchase a $100 gift for the past president."

If it becomes apparent to the presiding officer that there is need to create a blank, he/she may say, "It has become apparent that there is need to create a blank. If there are no objections a blank will be created. [Pause.] Hearing none, a blank has been

119

created." This maneuver (by member or chair) can be used when dates, places, names, figures, etc. are used in motions. It helps, in many instances, to expedite business.

RECONSIDER AND RESCIND

16a. *SOMETHING WAS VOTED ON EARLIER IN THIS MEETING BUT YOU HAVE NOW CHANGED YOUR MIND ABOUT YOUR VOTE*—What would you do?

16b. *THE MEETING ADJOURNED BEFORE YOU CHANGED YOUR MIND*—What would you do?

I refer to these as "the two Rs": RECONSIDER AND RESCIND.

One is used *at this meeting* and the other is used *after this meeting is over.* Both are attempts to undo something that has been done (adopted.) The motion to reconsider can be made *at this meeting only* and must be made by a member who voted on the prevailing (winning) side. The motion to rescind is made at a *later* meeting and can be made by any member, regardless of which side he/she voted on. Both motions require a majority vote; provided, that is, that members are given notice there will be an attempt to rescind. If notice is not given, then it will take a two-thirds vote, or a majority of the entire membership, to rescind a motion. The motion to reconsider always takes a majority vote to adopt.

After recognition by the presiding officer, you make a motion to reconsider.

Member: "Mister Chairman, I move that we reconsider the motion of ABC. The motion was adopted and I voted for the motion."

If the member had not announced that he/she had voted on the prevailing side, the chairman would ask, "Did the member vote on the prevailing side?" Upon proper assurance:

Chairman: "Is there a second? . . . A motion has been made and seconded that we reconsider the motion of ABC. Is there any discussion?"

The discussion must be limited to the reasons for reconsidering and cannot go into the merits of the main motion that you hope will be reconsidered. If the motion to reconsider is adopted, it merely means that the ABC item will come back again to the floor as if it had never been brought to a vote in the first place. The main motion will again be debated and another vote taken—the main motion is "getting a new trial." But the second vote could be the same as the first.

Despite the qualification that a motion to reconsider can only be made by a member who originally voted on the prevailing side, if the earlier vote was taken by secret ballot, anyone could then make the motion to reconsider.

For a rescinding, at a later meeting, obtain recognition from the presiding officer and make a motion to rescind.

Member: "Madam Chairman, I move that we rescind the action taken at our January meeting when we approved the expenditure of $50,000 for a summer swimming program."

Chairman: "Mister Treasurer, has any of this money already been spent or have we contracted to spend any of it yet?" [If so, then the motion cannot be rescinded.] "Since the money has not been spent and no contracts have been signed, the motion is in order. Is there a second? . . . a motion has been made and seconded that we rescind the action taken at our January meeting when we approved the expenditure of $50,000 for a summer swimming program. Is there any debate? . . . Since notice was given in our club newsletter, only a majority vote is required to adopt. All in favor say 'aye.' . . . Those opposed 'no.' . . . The motion is adopted and the January motion has been rescinded."

RESOLUTIONS

17. *YOU WANT TO PRESENT A CLEANUP PROJECT TO YOUR CLUB, BUT YOUR PROPOSAL HAS AT LEAST THREE DIFFERENT PARTS TO IT AND YOU MAY NOT GET RECOGNITION FROM THE CHAIRMAN THREE DIFFERENT TIMES TO PRESENT ALL OF THEM (RE-MEMBER, THERE ARE OTHERS AT YOUR MEETING WHO WANT TO PARTICIPATE TOO)*—What would you do?

Put the motion in the form of a RESOLUTION with WHEREAS and RESOLVING clauses. After recognition by the presiding officer, make the motion.

Member: "Madam Chairman, I move the adoption of the following resolution:

Whereas, for a number of years our city has won honors for being the cleanest city in the nation, and

Whereas, in the past few years we have been lax in our efforts to continue these honors, therefore

Be It Resolved, that our club sponsor a cleanup campaign through the schools, and

Be It Resolved, that we place waste cans in all shopping centers, and

Be It Further Resolved, that our members go to the parks each Sunday and collect all the rubbish."

Chairman: "Is there a second?" [If this motion had come from a committee a second would not be necessary, assuming, of course, that the committee consisted of more than one person.] "A motion has been made and seconded that the following resolution be adopted . . ." If each member has a copy of the resolution, the chairman will not be required to read the motion (resolution); but if there is any doubt that each member has heard it, the chairman must read it. Sometimes the chairman says, "May we consider the resolution just read, and of which you have copies, as the motion on the floor? Is there any discussion?" [Obviously, the resolution can be amended.] "All in favor say 'aye.' . . . Those opposed say 'no.' . . . The resolution is adopted."

DIVISION OF THE QUESTION—DEMAND DIVISION

18. *ANOTHER MEMBER HAS JUST MADE A SIMILAR PROPOSAL; THAT IS, WITH SEVERAL DIFFERENT PARTS TO IT, AND YOU LIKE SOME OF THEM BUT DO NOT LIKE OTHERS*—What would you do?

> If the items are distinctly different—in other words, each can be accomplished without being dependent on the others—you may simply state: "Mr. Chairman, I call for a separate vote on the items in the resolution." This is a demand and must be honored.

> If, however, you are considering a set of bylaws and want to consider each article separately before voting on them as a whole document, you may make a motion to consider them separately. After recognition by the presiding officer, state: "Mr. Chairman, I move that the bylaws be considered by articles." The motion must be seconded (S); it is not debatable, it is amendable (A), and it requires a majority (M) vote to adopt.

SUBSTITUTE MOTION

19. *A MEMBER HAS JUST BROUGHT UP A MOTION*

CONCERNING RECREATION FOR YOUR GROUP. YOU AGREE THAT RECREATION IS IN ORDER, BUT YOU DON'T AGREE WITH MANY OF THE DETAILS PRESENTED BY THIS MEMBER. YOU WANT TO CHANGE SEVERAL OF THE WORDS OR PHRASES IN THE PROPOSAL. IT APPEARS, HOWEVER, THAT TOO MUCH TIME WOULD BE SPENT IN CHANGING ALL OF THE WORDS YOU PROPOSE TO CHANGE. What would you do?

Rewrite the proposal in your own words and make a motion that your proposal be substituted for the one on the floor. After recognition by the chair, state:

Member: "Mister Chairman, I move that this document (paragraph, letter, etc.) be substituted for the document (paragraph, letter, etc.) that was presented in the main motion."

Chairman: "Is there a second? . . . A motion has been made and seconded to substitute the new document for the one that was presented in the main motion. The debate, which may include making amendments, will be first on the main motion (the first document), after which the debate, and possible amendments, will be on the substitute motion."

After the debate and amendments to each document (if there are any) have been properly voted on, the question will be: "All in favor of the substitute becoming the main motion say 'aye.' . . . Those opposed say 'no.' . . . The motion is adopted and the substitute motion has now become the main motion." Another vote must now be taken to see if the members accept the new main motion.

Keep in mind that when a substitute motion is made, it requires two votes: one vote determines whether the members want the main motion to remain as such or whether the members want the substitute motion to become the new main motion. It's as if you had two main motions on the floor

at the same time—which one do you like better?

After the members have decided which one they like better, that is, which one will become the new main motion, they then have to decide whether they want either one.

COMMITTEE OF THE WHOLE

20. *YOU ARE GOING TO PROPOSE A MATTER THAT IS CONTROVERSIAL AND YOU FEEL SURE SOME OF THE MEMBERS WILL TRY TO STOP THE DISCUS-SION, AS WELL AS USE OTHER MANEUVERS TO KILL IT, BEFORE IT CAN BE FULLY EXPLAINED AND DE-BATED. YOU ARE CONVINCED, HOWEVER, THAT IT IS OF SUCH IMPORTANCE TO THE COMMUNITY THAT A FULL AND COMPLETE HEARING SHOULD BE GIVEN THE PROPOSAL BEFORE IT IS ACTUALLY CONSIDERED BY FINAL VOTE.* What would you do?

Make a motion that the assembly go into a COM-MITTEE OF THE WHOLE to discuss this proposal. The requirements are similar to the motion to refer to committee; that is, it requires a second (S), it is debatable (D), it may be amended (A), and it requires a majority vote (M) to adopt. Usually the assembly goes into the committee of the whole immediately, so it would be too late to reconsider (R). If, however, the assembly does not go into the committee of the whole immediately, it may be reconsidered (R).

The purpose of the committee of the whole is to assure the assembly of full debate on *one* specific subject. Motions can be made in the committee of the whole; but the votes are not final. The assembly merely goes into committee-type (less formal) session to draft something that can be considered by the assembly when it returns to its regular meeting. No dilatory motions, such as close debate, table, or

125

any motion that prevents full debate of this one subject, can be made in the committee of the whole.

When the committee of the whole, having adopted a motion, returns to the regular meeting, the proposal is then open to all parliamentary maneuvers. The proposal now may be tabled, postponed, etc.

I have only seen the need for an assembly to go into the committee of the whole on one occasion, but then the need was definitely there. It involved a question that meant the possible change of the life-style, both physically and spiritually, of an international group of individuals. I served as their parliamentarian for one of the regional meetings, and then for their international convention.

They expressed their desire to have each person speak freely without anyone making any attempts to cut off the debate. The convention chairman presided during the committee of the whole and the group emerged with a "consensus" of what they wanted; the permanent chairman then resumed her position and the opponents of the question began their parliamentary maneuvering to kill it.

Before I explained the committee of the whole to them, they advised me that the time had come when they could no longer use parliamentary procedure to accomplish their purposes. I stated to them that I had *never* seen a situation where there wasn't a rule of common parliamentary law that couldn't assist a group in accomplishing the purposes for which it had assembled.

Part IV

THE CHAIRMAN

How to Proceed

You have just been elected, or appointed, to the top position in your organization. You may be referred to as the chairman, president, chairperson, chairwoman, chair, chairone, moderator, etc., but regardless of the title, the role is the same. How will you play this role? Will you perform your duties as a "leader" or a "driver"?

I ask this question because I constantly find individuals apparently confusing the two; they seem to feel that their role is to "drive their flock" rather than to "lead" them.

A definition for the word "lead," which is found in the *Webster New World Dictionary-College Edition* reads: " . . . to show the way or direct the course of, by going before, or along with; conduct, guide."

A definition for the word "driver" (found in the same dictionary) is: " . . . one who herds cattle." And, I frequently feel that I am supposed to play the role of one of the "herd." Do you?

Our country was founded by individuals who objected to being "subjects." They endured the hardships because they wanted to be free to govern themselves; to actively participate in their government. The first parliamentarian in this country was the man who composed the Declaration of Independence—the document which includes such rhetoric as "Liberty", yet the attitudes of many individuals are attitudesof servitude.

To be a *successful* chairman, and to have a *successful progressive organization*, you *must* assume that the organization belongs to the people who have paid their dues. If you are a political "leader," the dues-paying members are the taxpayers who put you into office. You must remember that you are the custodian of their affairs; the referee or the moderator. You are not the Master of the Flock, therefore, you are not capacle of running the show alone. As the president, you are not to assume the role as chairman of all committees, but the coordinator.

If there is a chairman of a committee who does not perform, you cannot guide and direct this chairman. It is your responsibility to guide the membership in such a manner that they recommend a replacement. You do not use your own initiative to relieve them of their duties, nor do you provide such weak leadership that such a member is allowed to remain in this position and do nothing.

I must assume that you feel your organization progresses only when the members are interested enough to become involved in its activities. In order for such involvement to become a reality, you must project the image of a leader who feels that each member is an important part of the organization. When organizations are structured in such a manner that a member can only have input if he or she is elected to the Board of Directors, such involvement will not be forthcoming.

Too many organizations have an Executive Committee meeting, a Board of Directors meeting, and a general membership meeting. The same people who attend the Executive Committee meeting and the meeting of the Board of Directors are also expected to attend the membership meeting—their third one. By the time the business comes before the members, if it does at all, it is already "cut and dried" and if a member dares ask a question, the inquiry becomes boring to those who have heard it twice before and the lonely member feels that he or she is a "troublemaker". What does he do then? Unless there is an item on the program that is of special interest, he doesn't attend the meetings and eventually fails to renew his membership. And, you wonder what happened!

I suspect that the reason most of the business of an organization or a political body is conducted by small groups—behind closed doors—is because the chairmen don't know how to handle the meetings where there are many opinions expressed. No one ever taught them how to conduct these meetings and they have not bothered to learn for themselves. The knowledge they need, of course, is the art of communicating in groups—parliamentary procedure. We know that such "closed door" meetings do exist, otherwise state legislative bodies would not have been forced, by the people, to enact the "Sunshine Laws", laws which assure open (public) meetings by elected officials.

How do you prepare yourself to preside at your meeting?

First, you must become as comfortable with "parliamentary procedure language" as you are with the words, "What's on television tonight?" This language is given to you in Parts I and II of this book. You must repeat this language until the words flow freely. If you are forced to hesitate simply because you are still unfamiliar with the "language", you have lost some of your leadership effectiveness.

As you preside, you must behave as though you are participating in the "Indianapolis 500 stock car races"; you cannot wait until the race begins before you find out where the steering wheel is located. You *do not practice* stating motions after your meetings begin. If you come to your meetings feeling comfortable with the "language" of parliamentary procedure, your mind will be free to grasp the intent of what the participants are trying to say or do at the meeting.

For example: A member will state: "Madam Chairman, I move that we TABLE this question until our next meeting." If you are too busy concentrating on whether the motion to Table needs a second, whether it is debatable, whether it requires a majority or ⅔ vote, or how you are going to state the motion, your mind will be too cluttered to realize that the motion was not stated properly or what the maker of the motion intended to say.

The motion to TABLE cannot be qualified, that is, you cannot state when the motion will be brought up again. The intent of this motion is to "POSTPONE the question to our next meeting" and not to TABLE IT.

If you have mastered the simple "language", and the information on the MOTIONS CHART, you will readily recognize the intent of the motion and guide the member accordingly. Do not "show off" your knowledge, but use it to expedite the business in an orderly, progressive, democratic manner, keeping it in mind that the minority shall be heard, but the majority shall rule. Do not be more technical than is absolutely necessary to accomplish these purposes.

If you are secure in your position as the presiding officer—and you will be if you follow the suggestions made above—you will have no problems in tactfully guiding the members who are not as secure. Instead of "correcting" the member who stated the motion wrong, you will simply state: "You are making the motion to 'postpone the question until the next meeting', right?" Usually the member will say "yes" or nod his or her head. If, however, the member insists on the motion as stated, you have no other choice but to rule the motion out of order, which brings me to my next point.

One of the most important aspects of being a good presiding officer is positive, but not arrogant, leadership. Forget that you have friends or enemies in the assembly. *You have no friends or enemies at the time you are presiding.* You are the referee or the moderator at this meeting. You may resume your friendship, or fight, whichever the case may be, after the meeting is over.

You must not be sensitive; you must be impartial. You must make decisions without hesitation, always with the attitude that the members of the assembly can appeal your decision. Don't hesitate saying, "The Chair stands corrected," if you are wrong.

Frankly, I welcome appeals. An "appeal from the decision of the chair" simply means that a member has a question about the manner in which a situation has been handled and, instead of keeping the telephone lines busy after the meeting, or discussing it "over the backyard fence", welcome the fact that the issue is being questioned at the meeting. If you, the chairman, and the member do not come to an agreement, the members of the assembly decide the issue. The responsibility has now been placed on the members. What could be healthier for your organization?

Most organizations have a parliamentarian. I have found that most member parliamentarians don't know any more about procedure than you do. The majority of members, however, are of the opinion that if a member holds the title of "parliamentarian," that that member is an authority and should rule on issues. Nothing could be further from the truth. First, unless there is someone who is knowledgeable of the subject, do not have a parliamentarian. There is no rule that states a parliamentarian must be appointed. It is an excellent idea, however, provided you can find a good one. It is also better to have a parliamentarian who is not a member of your group; opinions will be assumed to be more objective. PARLIAMEN—TARIANS DO NOT RULE, THEY ONLY GIVE OPINIONS. You, the Chairman or presiding officer, rule on all questions, subject to appeals from members of the assembly.

Do not hesitate to use the term, "If there are no objections . . ."

For example: It appears to you that the majority of the members are bored with the debate. Only a few individuals are debating the issue and each debate is becoming increasingly repetitious. You simply state: "If there are no objections, we will limit the debate on this question to only three more minutes." Pause long enough to give the members the opportunity to object. Or, if it is obvious that the members are getting restless, you may say: "If there are no objections, we will have a ten minute recess." You must pause, however, to be certain that the members have the time to object if they do not agree. If a member does object, then you can do no more. You must wait for motions to come from the floor.

Under no circumstances should you fall into the "Question" trap. That is, when a member calls out "Question", expecting you to bring the motion to an immediate vote. Presiding officers who fall into this trap will state: "The question has been called for and we must vote. All in favor. . . ."

The intent of the "Question Caller" is to make a motion to "Close Debate." Such a motion requires recognition by the chairman. Calling out "Question" is out of order because the member needs to be recognized by the chair. The motion requires seconding and a ⅔ vote is required—twice as many voting affirmatively as those voting negatively. If a member calls out "Question," you may simply state: "Are you making a motion to close debate?" If the member says "yes", ask for a second and put the question to an immediate vote.

Seven Rules for Becoming an Effective Chairman (Presiding Officer)

1. Always have a gavel.
2. Always have an agenda prepared.
3. Always assume the role of the referee, moderator, co-ordinator and/or custodian.
4. Always be aware that the organization belongs to the members and is not your personal property.
5. Always treat all members equally—as if the organization would not be the same without them.
6. Always be aware that simple parliamentary procedure rules and terminology must be learned and practiced until they become a part of your everyday vocabulary.
7. Always apply the rules that you have learned with a great deal of common sense and logic, using the strictness of the rules only when it is necessary to accomplish your goals for an orderly, progressive, productive, democratic meeting.

Part V

GLOSSARY

Ad hoc: (literally—for this purpose; special) Usually used when describing a committee. An ad hoc committee is one appointed for a special task and is automatically discharged when it has completed its assigned task.

Adjourn: To end a meeting, either for one day or indefinitely.

Adjourn cum die: If a day is scheduled for the next session or meeting, the adjournment is referred to as cum die. These meetings are usually those scheduled less than three months ahead.

Adjourn sine die: If the meetings (such as annual conventions) are set so that more than three moths will elapse the adjournments are sine die.

Adopt: To vote to accept (a committee report, motion, resolution, etc.)

Agenda: A list of things to be done or dealt with (as at a meeting).

Amend: To change an item by adding, striking, or striking and inserting a word or words.

Appeal: A member's refusal to accept the chair's ruling unless the organization concurs. It is based on the challenger's belief that the presiding officer made a parliamentary error.

Board: A group of members (sometimes including non-member experts) appointed or elected to coordinate the work of the organization. The authority given a board is determined in the organization's bylaws.

Budget: An advance statement of anticipated income and expected expenses.

Bylaws: The rules by which an organization is to be governed.

Caucus: An informal session (off the record) of a group of members, held in order to agree on tactics, candidates, or policies.

Chair: The presiding officer—a position of authority.

Chairman: The presiding officer or leader of a group of people.

Charter: A franchise or written grant of specified rights made by a government or ruler to a person, business corporation, etc. Permission from a society for the organization of a local chapter.

Commit: To refer to a committee or board.

Committee: A group of people chosen to consider some matter or to function in a certain capacity.

Committee of the Whole: An informal meeting of all members of the organization who are present. It is an off-the-record-type meeting with a new chairman presiding. There shall be no dilatory motions made at such meeting, and no votes taken are final.

Constitution: The fundamental document that broadly outlines the purpose and structure of the organization. If the organization is given its life by a "charter," the charter is, in effect, the constitution. The law of the organization.

Convene: To meet together.

Convention: An assembly, often periodic, of members or their elected representatives.

Credential: An identifying document that a member carries when named as a delegate, observer, or representative.

Debate: To discuss opposing reasons.

Dilatory: Causing delay. Any motion that may delay the main motion is called a dilatory motion.

Division of the House (Division): A demand for a clarification of the vote; a standing vote.

Division of the Question: Dividing a long motion, resolution, or bylaw provisions into parts so that they can be considered separately.

Executive Session: Exclusion of nonmembers.

Ex officio: (literally—by virtue of office) Entitlement to a position solely because of holding some other office. For example, the bylaws provide that the mayor of the city shall be an ex officio member. Regardless of who the mayor happens to be, he or she is automatically a member.

Fiscal Year: The financial year of an organization.

Floor: In front of the assembly. A motion to be considered is on the "floor." A person who has been properly recognized to speak has the "floor."

General Consent: Unanimous agreement is inferred simply because no one has objected.

General Order: An item that was postponed to 2:00 P.M. today is a general order and will be taken up at 2:00 P.M., after the matter on the floor at that time is disposed of. (Special Order is one that will be taken up at 2:00 P.M. regardless of what is on the floor at that time.)

Incidental Motion: A motion made while another matter is pending (on the floor), but that does not directly dispose of the main motion.

Information, Point of: The method by which a member may seek an immediate answer to a question concerning the content or background of a motion.

Inquiry (Parliamentary), Point of: The method by which a member may seek an immediate answer to a question concerning the procedure being used at the meeting.

Lay on the Table: To place a main motion and all subsidiary motions attached to it in the secretary's book. If a member wishes to bring the motion back (Take from the Table) and place it on the floor for further consideration, he/she may do so, but only after one intermediate item of business has been transacted and before the adjournment of the following meeting. A *motion is required* to Lay on the Table and also to Take from the Table.

Main Motion: An idea that has been placed on the floor for consideration by the membership.

Majority: More than half of those voting. If there are 100 members present at a meeting and only five members vote, the majority would be three votes. Those who do not vote are not counted in the majority. A majority means a majority of those votes cast.

Meeting: A meeting occurs whenever a quorum of members engages in parliamentary activities. An "annual meeting" or "convention" describes a whole series; a single sitting is a "session."

Moderator: A chairman of a session, or the "referee."

Motion: A proposal for action. A verbal proposal is referred to as a motion, while a written proposal is called a resolution.

Object to Consideration: A parliamentary maneuver that must be made before one word of debate has begun on the idea (the motion). When the debate has begun, the assembly is, in fact, considering the motion.

Old Business: (see Unfinished Business).

Orders of the Day: An agenda that the assembly has adopted. "Call for the Orders of the Day" is a demand that the agenda be followed.

Parliamentary Inquiry: (see Inquiry [Parliamentary], Point of).

Pending: The matter that is on the floor.

Plurality: The largest number of votes cast when you have three or more choices. Example:
>A receives 50 votes
>B receives 100 votes
>C receives 57 votes. No one received a majority of all votes cast, but B received a plurality (more than any other).

Point of Information: (see Information, Point of).

Precedence: Rank of motions (see Rank).

Previous Question: A term that means "close debate."

Primary Motion: Same as main motion.

Privilege: The right to immediate consideration of a matter that affects the safety, orderliness, or comfort of the members, or that affects the honor of an individual member.

Proxy: A signed paper that authorizes a person to cast the signer's vote. An instructed proxy is one where the signer has instructed the authorized person how to cast his vote, while an uninstructed proxy has no limitations.

Putting the Question: The call for the vote; "All in favor say 'aye,' etc."

Quorum: The smallest number legally capable of doing

business. A quorum is a majority of the entire membership unless otherwise stated in the bylaws. Regardless of the size of an organization a quorum should never be more than 100 members. Keep the figure as low as possible to assure a representative assembly.

Rank: The rank of a motion is its claim to right of way over another motion. Thus, a motion to adjourn has a higher rank than a motion to postpone (see chart).

Ratify: To approve or confirm a motion, resolution, etc.

Recess: A brief interruption in a session. When the session resumes after a recess, all matters are in the same parliamentary position as they were just before the recess.

Recognize: To take notice of and give the floor to (implying the right to speak) by the presiding officer. This may be done by the chairman calling out the member's name, pointing or nodding to him, or otherwise signaling that he/she may speak.

Reconsider: To review again a matter previously disposed of, and to vote on it again. The motion is "getting a new trial."

Rescind: To nullify or cancel out a previous action.

Resolution: A written motion; a proposal reduced to writing, phrased in a special style with "whereas" and resolving clauses (see Resolving Clause).

Resolving Clause: The second part of a resolution. The first is the "whereas," or reason for the resolution, and the second part is the resolving or what you plan to do about it.

Roll Call Vote: A recorded vote taken by calling the roll of the membership.

Second a Motion: To add one's voice to that of the maker of a motion.

Secondary Motion: A proposal to do something to a main motion—to amend the main motion; to postpone it; to table it (see chart). Also called Subsidiary Motion.

Session: A meeting terminated by adjournment cum die. The word means a sitting. A one session, 3 meeting convention.

Session, Executive: (see Executive Session).

Show of Hands: Voting by raising hands; "All in favor of this motion, raise your hand...."

Speaker: A spokesman—the chairman of a group may be the "speaker" for the group; the presiding officer of a deliberative assembly.

Special Order: A matter that has been postponed to a specific time and stated as a "special order" is automatically brought to the floor when that hour and minute arrives. Anything else on the floor must step aside. A special order requires a two-thirds vote because it does impose upon the normal rights of others, e.g., that individual who had the floor at that particular time.

146

Standing Committee: A committee that has a predetermined area of jurisdiction and handles all matters that fall within that area; a committee with a term that coincides with that of officers.

Standing Vote: A rising vote; "All in favor of the motion, please stand. . . ."

Stating the Question: Stating the motion or advising the group what the idea is that is on the floor. "Question" is synonymous with "motion."

Subsidiary Motion: (see Secondary Motion).

Suspension of the Rules: To change the order of the adopted agenda. This requires a two-thirds vote.

Table, Lay on: (see Lay on the Table).

Take from the Table: (see Lay on the Table).

Teller: A person named to count the votes.

Two-thirds Vote: Twice as many voting "affirmatively" as those voting "negatively." There are 100 members present, but only 15 voted. If ten voted "yes" and five voted "no," the motion was adopted by a two-thirds vote.

Unfinished Business: A matter that was pending at a previous meeting, but not disposed of; questions that were unfinished business at the previous meeting, but were not reached before adjournment; and any questions that were postponed as general orders.

Voice Vote: (viva voce—by word of mouth; orally). When the chairman calls, "All in favor say 'aye,' " he/she is calling for a voice vote. It is measured by appraising loudness of the "aye" and "no" responses.